T0039652

# Hmong
## IN WISCONSIN

## Mai Zong Vue

WISCONSIN HISTORICAL SOCIETY PRESS

Published by the Wisconsin Historical Society Press
*Publishers since 1855*

The Wisconsin Historical Society helps people connect to the past
by collecting, preserving, and sharing stories. Founded in 1846,
the Society is one of the nation's finest historical institutions.
*Join the Wisconsin Historical Society:* wisconsinhistory.org/membership

Front cover: Faith Lo and Lillian Vang at a Hmong New Year celebration in Madison
in November of 2017. Photo by Mai Zong Vue.

Images are from the collection of Mai Zong Vue unless otherwise noted.

Printed in Wisconsin, USA
Designed by Jane Tenenbaum

24  23  22  21  20     1  2  3  4  5

Library of Congress Cataloging-in-Publication Data
Names: Vue, Mai Zong, author.
Title: Hmong in Wisconsin / Mai Zong Vue.
Description: Madison : Wisconsin Historical Society Press, [2020] | Includes
bibliographical references and index. | Summary: "One of Wisconsin's more recent
immigrant groups, the Hmong were recruited by the CIA to fight communists in their
home country of Laos during the Secret War of the 1960s and 1970s. When Saigon
fell in 1975, the surviving Hmong had to flee for their lives, ending up in refugee
camps in Thailand for many years before being relocated to the United States and
other countries. Wisconsin is now home to the third largest Hmong population in the
country, following California and Minnesota. Told with a mixture of scholarly
research and personal experience of the author, who grew up in a Thai refugee camp,
Hmong in Wisconsin shares the story of this perilous journey and the Hmong's
experiences adapting to life in Wisconsin communities"— Provided by publisher.
Identifiers: LCCN 2019034395 | ISBN 9780870209420 (paperback) |
ISBN 9780870209437 (e-book)
Subjects: LCSH: Vue, Mai Zong, author. | Hmong (Asian people)—Wisconsin. |
Hmong Americans—Wisconsin. | Refugees—Wisconsin.
Classification: LCC F590.H55 V84 2020 | DDC 975.5/00495972—dc23 LC record
available at https://lccn.loc.gov/2019034395

*I would like to dedicate this book to all Hmong parents and community leaders who resettled in Wisconsin and whose hard work, refugee experience, and legacy are worth preserving; to the children of Hmong descendants in Wisconsin, for whom this book is an introduction to your heritage; and to the people of Wisconsin, who welcomed us as new Americans.*

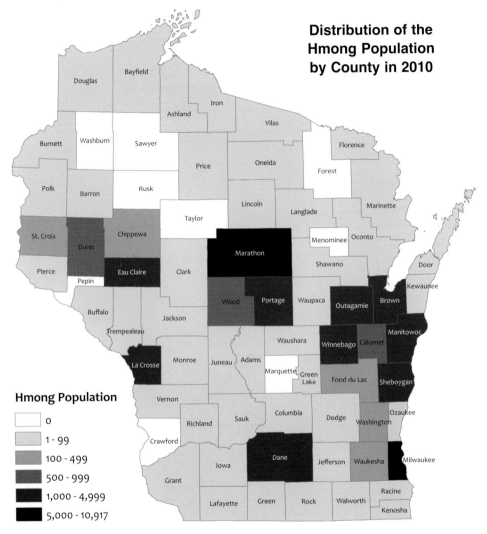

# Distribution of the Hmong Population by County in 2010

**Hmong Population**

- 0
- 1 - 99
- 100 - 499
- 500 - 999
- 1,000 - 4,999
- 5,000 - 10,917

UW Applied Population Laboratory and Extension

# INTRODUCTION

*Our journey to the United States was scary and long.*
*We did not know where our final destination was going to be*
*or whom we would meet once we got there. The journey began*
*when our family of five took a bus from Ban Vinai to Bangkok.*
*Once in Bangkok we waited for a few more days to complete our*
*medical screenings and paperwork. Then we flew to O'Hare airport*
*in Chicago. A Catholic church had sponsored our family to the*
*United States. I remember feeling anxious and lost. There was a lot*
*of noise at the airport, and we did not know which way to go once*
*we came out of the plane. When we saw a Caucasian man holding*
*a piece of cardboard with the name "Xiong" on it, we knew we*
*were in the right place.*

With these words, Kaying Xiong recalled the anxiety and uncertainty of
her family's refugee journey for an essay project conducted by artist and
writer Kou Vang. Unlike earlier immigrant groups who came to Wisconsin in search of economic opportunities that would lead to a better
life, the Hmong arrived in the state as political refugees after fleeing for
their lives from their home country of Laos. After many years of war, in
which many Hmong fought alongside other Laotian ethnic groups to
keep communism from taking over their country and assisted the Americans in the Vietnam War, the country fell under control of the Communist Pathet Lao.

As the Pathet Lao began to retaliate against their opponents, the
Hmong were in danger of being captured, tortured, and killed. Survivors
faced dwindling food and medical supplies, and villages filled with the
cries of sick and hungry children. Those who remained faced a terrible
choice: continuing the struggle to survive in worsening circumstances, or
leaving their homeland to try to follow General Vang Pao and other
Hmong leaders who had evacuated to Thailand. Some elders refused to
abandon their homes. But many quickly gathered whatever belongings
they could carry and began their long journey on foot, embarking on the
difficult march from the hills of Laos to Thailand.

Over many days, the Hmong ate whatever roots or edible greens they found on their way to the Mekong River, the border dividing Laos and Thailand. They traveled as silently as possible, using opium to quiet babies and young children, many of whom died as a result of the drug. The first few thousand Hmong to reach the Thai side of the Mekong were greeted by Thai farmers with food. As their numbers grew into the tens of thousands, however, later refugees were victimized by Thai soldiers who stole their jewelry, money, or other personal belongings.

Thai refugee camps became overcrowded within months. Many slept in open fields or among tall weeds for months, awaiting the construction of shelters or tents, before moving to the comparative luxury of a nine-by-nine-foot room meant to house an entire family. An intake camp was established at what is now the Thai city of Nong Khai, located about twenty kilometers from Vientiane, Laos, on the southern bank of the Mekong River. Refugees would stay at Nong Khai for several weeks until the Thai government determined where to send them for the long term. By 1977, about twenty-two thousand Lao, Hmong, and Lao-Vietnamese refugees had found their way to Nong Khai, according to *A People's History of the Hmong*. Ban Vinai Refugee Camp in northeast Thailand held the largest number of Hmong refugees, reaching forty-five thousand at one time. Many Hmong refugees moved from camp to camp, not knowing what the future held for themselves or for their children. They waited months and sometimes even years, hoping for a safe return to Laos or for resettlement opportunities elsewhere.

Because of US involvement in recruiting and leading the Hmong fighters against the Communists in Laos and the aid of the Hmong people in the US Vietnam War effort, the United States ended up accepting the vast majority of the refugees. About thirty-five hundred Hmong refugees, mostly high-level military commanders and their families, had been relocated to the United States by December 1975. Wisconsin's first arrivals, sponsored by Catholic Charities Diocese and Lutheran Social Services, arrived on January 31, 1976. The two families, those of Xia Vang and Tou Her, spoke some English and used hand gestures to communicate with their American benefactors, because no Hmong interpreters were available during the early waves of refugee resettlement.

Wisconsin had received 408 Hmong refugees by 1980, after which the rate of resettlement increased dramatically, with almost seventeen thousand Hmong calling Wisconsin home by 1990, according to *The Atlas of Ethnic Diversity in Wisconsin*. Just like the war effort in Laos, the Hmong's arrival in Wisconsin attracted little attention from the American public at first. Knowledge of the Hmong and their recent history in Southeast Asia was largely limited to a network of church sponsors and government officials. Moreover, federal refugee policies scattered the Hmong across more than fifteen counties in Wisconsin, straining the important Hmong clan system. By the end of the twentieth century, Hmong communities could be found in cities including Milwaukee, Madison, Wausau, La Crosse, Eau Claire, Chippewa Falls, Green Bay, Sheboygan, Appleton, Neenah, Manitowoc, Two Rivers, Stevens Point, Oshkosh, Fond du Lac, Ladysmith, Mauston, Superior, Tomah, and Menomonie.

Today, Wisconsin is home to the third-largest Hmong population in the United States, after California and Minnesota. As of 2010, Wisconsin had 49,240 Hmong, of whom 20,676 were foreign born, according to census data. Although arriving much more recently than other immigrant groups, many Hmong families are well established by this point, with nearly half arriving prior to 1990. Fifty-five percent of Wisconsin's Hmong population owned their own homes in 2010. The Hmong population in America is both young and growing, with a median age of 20.2 as of the 2010 Census.

This book shares the story of the Hmong in Wisconsin. It includes a combination of historical background and Hmong resettlement stories, including my own. Born in Laos during the Vietnam War, I was seven when the Hmong fled Laos, and my family spent five years living in Na Phong and Ban Vinai Thai refugee camp. We arrived in Illinois in 1980 through a church sponsor and then relocated to Wisconsin after two weeks to join my older sister's family, who had arrived in 1976. After growing up in Laos, Thailand, and Wisconsin, I became the first college graduate in my family. I then worked for the Wisconsin State Refugee Office for twenty years as a refugee program specialist. I also led the Refugee Women's Initiative in Wisconsin and served as board president of Hmong National Development, an organization that promotes economic prosperity in the Hmong community through education, leadership training, research, and policy advocacy. In addition to experiencing firsthand the difficult journey the Hmong made from Laos to the United

States, I have shared in the challenges and successes of many other Hmong families who have made their homes in Wisconsin through my work in the refugee office and my involvement in the state's Hmong community. For this project, seeking to offer a more complete range of experiences, I also conducted many interviews and gathered information from scholarly and other sources.

Among the many important issues explored in the book are Hmong acculturation and assimilation experiences. Challenges facing Hmong religious practices, employment, education, and business development are highlighted, as are the specific issues relevant to Hmong elders and women today. It is my great hope that this book will inspire and encourage people, including the descendants of Hmong refugees, to read and learn more about the Hmong way of life and their experiences in Wisconsin. The Hmong have made many contributions in their time as Wisconsinites, which also deserve mention for their merits and for their significance to the history of the Badger State.

## FROM CHINA TO LAOS

True citizens of the world, the Hmong people can be found in China, Laos, Vietnam, Thailand, Burma, the United States, Australia, Canada, France, Germany, and many other countries. Though scholars have debated the origins of the Hmong people, their history can be traced going back at least four thousand years to China. In addition to Chinese records that seem to refer to the Hmong, the Hmong have their own rich oral tradition that informs their origins and lineage. It is common for Hmong elders to tell their grandchildren ancient stories about the journey from China to Southeast Asia—a story that includes a civilized society led by a king. According to Hmong oral stories, the Hmong have their roots near the Huang He (Yellow) and the Yangtze Rivers in China. In autonomous kingdoms, the Hmong grew rice on flat land using rice paddy techniques. According to Guodong Li, a scholar at Hiroshima University, the Hmong were the creators of rice culture, spreading an agricultural way of life centered on rice to the lower reaches of the Yangtze River, to the lower reaches of the Korean peninsula, and finally to the Japanese archipelago.

Oral stories and written texts suggest that the Hmong faced frequent attacks from the Chinese as the Hmong and imperial China fought for control of valuable land. Dr. Yang Dao, a prominent Hmong historian, wrote, "Generally peaceable, but with a wild, proud spirit of independence...the Hmong people pulled up stakes from imperialist China under expansionist pressure of the Han, and ahead of massacres of their members." The Chinese coined the terms *cooked* to refer to Hmong whom they were able to force to assimilate and *raw* for Hmong who resisted assimilation and relocated to remote mountain areas to better defend themselves. After a series of unsuccessful rebellions against Chinese control, thousands of raw Hmong migrated to Vietnam, Laos, Thailand, and Myanmar, no longer able to tolerate life under the Chinese emperors.

The Hmong gradually migrated throughout Southeast Asia from 1810 to 1820. My great-great-grandfather was among the raw Hmong who walked for months in search of a new life. The journey to Southeast Asia from China was tough; oral stories documented by Doua H. Vu in *Remembering the Hmong* state that due to starvation, some Hmong families were forced to trade a child for three *ncuav pias* (wheat patties). While some stayed in Vietnam, others kept going, reaching Laos, Thailand, or Myanmar. In Laos, as the lowland was occupied with Laotian and other ethnic groups, the Hmong went up into the mountains to avoid making new enemies and to live in cooler altitudes, as they were unaccustomed to the intense heat. There, they briefly clashed with the native Khmu people over the Khmu's increasing demands for opium in exchange for use of the lands. The Hmong, who had brought superior weapons from China, drove most of the Khmu out of the area and negotiated peace with those who remained. Over the years, the Hmong reestablished a life of simple farming, maintaining their own traditions, language, and cultural identity separate from other Laotians.

The Hmong have eighteen clans, with membership determined by birth or adoption. Although women belong to the clan of their husbands upon marriage, both men and women carry their clan names for life. Hmong villages consist of one to three clans, each with their own leader. Clans are further divided into households of Hmong who share a close familial bond, or *ib tsev neeg*. Households typically include a nuclear family, along with other extended family members. Clans relied on a system of cooperative farming for efficiency and to maintain a strong community. Family roles were clearly defined by gender, age, kinship, and clanship.

Life was largely peaceful until the French began to colonize Laos in 1893. The French imposed heavy taxes, which the Hmong had to pay in addition to the annual taxes and tributes that they had already been paying to Laotian authorities. The amounts totaled more than the yearly earnings of many Hmong households. When the French sent a militia to enforce the tax, the Hmong organized and attacked. Although the Hmong feared they would be imprisoned or put to death over the rebellion, the French negotiated terms that would allow the Hmong to pay their taxes in livestock and opium, which could be easily grown in the high mountainous areas they occupied, and which became a significant source of revenue for the French. In 1918, Pachay Vue, considered a hero in Hmong history, led another rebellion against the French. After a bloody three-year conflict that ended in the assassination of Pachay Vue and other clan leaders who supported him, the French granted the Hmong more autonomy and recognition.

## WAR IN LAOS

When the Japanese briefly occupied Laos during World War II, some Hmong allied themselves with the French resistance. In 1945, the French regained control of Laos, setting it up as a constitutional monarchy within the French Union and awarding the Royal Laotian government limited powers. Leaders of a national movement, the Pathet Lao, allied themselves with the Vietminh, the Communist movement that formed in 1941 to fight French rule in Vietnam. Through guerrilla warfare, the Pathet Lao and Vietminh took control of two northern provinces of Laos in 1953, then defeated the French military at the Battle of Dien Bien Phu in 1954. Later that year, the Geneva Accord established Laos as a neutral country and ordered all foreign powers to withdraw.

The US government disagreed with the result of the Geneva Accord, viewing Laos as an important front to prevent the spread of communism from China and North Vietnam into South Vietnam, Cambodia, and Thailand. The weakness of Laos's central government and the poverty of its people made it especially vulnerable to communism without outside help, so the United States provided economic and military aid. In 1960, after the Communists of the Pathet Lao staged a successful coup in Laos, the Soviet Union started supporting them. As a result, two foreign superpowers became involved in Laos, an adjacent conflict to the Vietnam War.

The United States limited its involvement in Laos to covert CIA operations to avoid directly engaging with the Soviet Union, in a conflict that came to be known as the Secret War. The CIA worked with Hmong leader Vang Pao and financed and equipped Hmong guerrilla units to support the Royal Laotian Army. US operatives recruited the Hmong by emphasizing the threat of Vietnamese encroachment on their land and the role the US would play in helping them to defend their homes. Thousands of Hmong answered the call. Many of Vang Pao's soldiers were eager to join the fight against Communism. The small salaries they received helped to support their families after many of the Hmong's formerly self-reliant farming communities had been displaced by fighting. In *A Brief History of the Hmong and the Secret War in Laos*, Steve Schofield writes, "In 1960, the CIA supplied the Hmong with small arms. The CIA recruited, trained, fed, paid, and equipped the Hmong to fight the North Vietnamese Army." In addition to guerrilla warfare, the Hmong performed several critical duties that helped the US war effort in Vietnam. The first was to protect the crucial US landing and navigational site known as Lima Site 85 that guided the B-52 bombers and other US fighter aircraft over North Vietnamese airspace. The second and more dangerous job was to rescue downed American pilots from the jungles of North Vietnam. Late in the war, the CIA trained several Hmong fighter pilots who provided air support. This operation was conducted without the knowledge or consent of Congress and was kept secret from the American people from 1954 to 1969, when a Senate committee convened hearings on US involvement in Laos.

By 1968, anti-Communists were losing ground both in Laos and Vietnam. In the early 1970s, the United States started withdrawing its support, but Hmong soldiers continued to fight for their survival. Over a span of fifteen years of fighting, an estimated thirty thousand Hmong died, including many civilian casualties due to grenades, land mines, hunger, and disease. Hmong boys as young as twelve had been recruited to fight in the Secret Army, and many lost their lives. Nhia Thong "Charles" Lor survived the fighting and now lives in Madison. "I lost my father and uncle in the war," he recalled. "I, too, almost lost my life. I fought hard and did everything I was told as a young boy, so young I could not carry an M-16." WaSeng Ly of Appleton worked at the direction of the CIA during the Secret War, directing American pilots toward their targets in North Vietnam. When pilots went down, Ly said, it was not unusual for two or three Hmong men to die during the rescue effort. Ly himself was injured in the head. He still has a bullet fragment in his left brain, and his right hand is permanently paralyzed.

As a result of the Secret War, Hmong children such as me grew up in a war-torn country. During the war, the Hmong in Laos lived like prisoners in our own homes. While the men were at war, those left behind moved and hid when enemies attacked our villages. The lack of labor and pressure to stay on the move made farming difficult. When the United States Aid for International Development (USAID) airdropped rice and canned goods, we scrambled to claim what we could. Those who tried to maintain a normal life of farming and raising animals often never got to harvest their crops or use their livestock. Many families relocated to Long Chieng, a town and air base where the CIA had set up operations. Long Chieng came to house more than forty thousand Hmong at one time. Children born during the Secret War knew nothing of a peaceful life. We lived instead in constant fear of the next attack.

In 1973, a ceasefire agreement established a coalition government and expelled all foreign military units from the country. But once Cambodia and South Vietnam fell in 1975, the Pathet Lao pushed for a total takeover of the Laotian government and began retaliating against the Hmong and others who had opposed them. Hmong leaders and soldiers who had fought on the side of the Americans were arrested, tortured, and killed. A group of Hmong who came to be known as the ChaoFa fled into the jungle to hide. Forced to move constantly from place to place to avoid detection, the ChaoFa were unable to raise crops or build shelters. They lacked access to clean drinking water, adequate food, or medical care.

## THE REFUGEE JOURNEY

After the fall of Saigon, the United States withdrew the rest of its ground forces from Southeast Asia and airlifted about twenty-five hundred Hmong soldiers, including General Vang Pao and other high-ranking military leaders, out of the country. The remaining Hmong experienced genocidal retribution for their role in opposing the Pathet Lao. Word spread of a mass shooting in Hin Heup, where Communist soldiers shot, injured, and killed hundreds of Hmong who were trying to leave the country through the capital, Vientiane. Bao Vang of Mauston, later a regular vendor at the farmers' market at the Capitol Square in Madison, was a victim in this mass shooting. For the Hmong in Wisconsin, Bao's uneven and scarred face became a living testimony of the violence the Hmong faced following the war. Bao described the incident to me in 2013: "I was young and just got married. My parent-in-law said everyone must leave together the next day, so we did. I witnessed two family members died that day. It happened so quickly as we marched forward toward the bridge. My uncle on my right side was shot and fell to the ground. Then a bullet went through my son-in-law's forehead, out his left ear, and sliced my left face. My son-in-law fell in front of me. Both of them died while we carried them."

While some stayed behind and tried to survive in Laos, others began the long journey by foot to Thailand. They crossed the heavily patrolled Mekong River under cover of night, entering the dangerously strong currents on crude rafts made from tied-together banana tree trunks, tire tubes, and bamboo. Those who could not swim tied themselves to other family members. Some parents kept their children quiet with opium; some even let their babies drown or left them behind if it would help the group avoid detection. Many did not survive, dying of starvation or illness, being captured by the Pathet Lao, or drowning in the fast-moving currents of the Mekong during monsoon season. Some were robbed of a proper burial. Mothers in my Wisconsin Refugee Women's Project have told horrifying stories of parents tying their exhausted children to tree trunks, hoping that others would save them. The bodies of children who died along the way were covered with only a few banana leaves. Some families properly grieved their losses, while many others did not have the time or chance to do the same and never found relief from their guilt.

The dangerous journey left emotional scars. Vayong Moua of Eau Claire, a baby in 1975, was among the lucky ones to make it across the river. He reflected on the experience with his friends and colleagues during the former refugees' thirty-fourth anniversary in Wisconsin: "I jokingly told my parents they were reckless to have two kids on the run from Communist soldiers, anchoring them back in a refugee camp, and at the ultimate precipice of uncertainty. My mother quietly and sternly responded, 'Having you and VaMeng were the only things that kept us going. Otherwise, giving up would've been easier.'"

The Hmong sought safety and refuge in Thailand from 1975 to 2004, arriving in three main phases: those who left Laos directly following the Communist takeover, those who fled the government's violent crackdown on Hmong soldiers, and the later refugees driven out by worsening economic conditions. The Hmong who did not meet the refugee eligibility criteria set by the United Nations went into hiding, gradually assimilated into Thai society, or returned to Laos. Those accepted as refugees in Thailand awaited relocation opportunities in America, Australia, French Guiana, France, and other European countries.

While recruiting Hmong soldiers to fight the spread of communism in Southeast Asia, American operatives working in Laos had assured the Hmong that they would be safely relocated if they lost the war. Many Hmong fought on the side of the Americans with the belief that the United States would accept them as refugees afterward if their home country became unsafe. Some Hmong leaders recalled verbal promises made to them and felt they deserved the help as recognition for their services. Neng Yee Kong of Green Bay, a business owner and former USAID employee, described a personal message he received from a USAID worker following the war: "Two days after I arrived in the refugee camp, my supervisor, Bill Sage, had someone deliver a note to me. I did not know what it was. I opened it and it read: 'Yee, I feel very sorry you lost your country, but I will find a sponsor for you. Signed, Bill Sage.'"

Although the United States did end up involving itself in the relocation of refugees, the US government was slow to do so. Because the CIA's involvement in Laos was unofficial and had been kept secret from the American people, the US State Department did not have an official policy in place at the end of the Secret War to accept the Laotian refugees. Per the Indochina Refugee and Migration Act passed in 1975, the United States was officially accepting only Indochinese refugees from Vietnam and Cambodia at that time. Additionally, some at the state department voiced the view that the Hmong were too primitive and would not be able to succeed in an industrial society. After Hmong leaders and US supporters lobbied Congress to include Laotians, Hmong refugees were officially accepted beginning in January 1976. Later, the Refugee Act of 1980 created the Office of Refugee Resettlement (ORR), which worked with state agencies and private sponsors, mostly churches, to place refugees.

## HMONG RESETTLEMENT EXPERIENCES IN WISCONSIN

People often ask me why the Hmong came to Wisconsin, a cold place very different from Laos. But Wisconsin was suitable in several important ways: the education system, the existence of employment opportunities, and the availability of sponsors, many of them connected to churches or faith-based organizations, who stepped up to welcome the new arrivals and help them adjust to their new lives.

Sponsors greeted the Hmong refugees at the airport with blankets and coats for those who arrived in the dead of winter. Despite the language barrier, friendly and warm smiles were exchanged among most Hmong refugees and their sponsors. Church sponsors knew little about the Hmong refugee families, especially their language and culture. Some sponsors did not even know the difference between a Hmong and Vietnamese refugee; they often brought a Vietnamese interpreter to greet Hmong families at the airport. The assumption was, according to Father Robert Paul Vandenberg of St. Paul Catholic Church in Kimberly, that because the refugees were a product of the Vietnam War, they must be Vietnamese.

Many Hmong parents and elders, including my father, came to Wisconsin fearful of what to expect. They did not know if Americans would welcome them or turn them away. Their understandable fear of the unknown prompted many to prolong their time in the refugee camps.

Upon arrival, the Hmong's experiences were bittersweet. While many of those who sponsored the Hmong embraced the refugees, most Wisconsinites knew nothing of the Hmong or why they had come to America. Stigmas and cultural misunderstandings in the years that followed led to verbal abuse, racial discrimination, and even a few incidents of violence.

Like many Hmong families, my family enjoyed a honeymoon stage upon our arrival in Wisconsin. During our honeymoon stage, most of us were welcomed, sheltered, and protected in our sponsors' homes. Our sponsors accepted our cultural differences and patiently taught us what we needed to know, such as how to find work, how to enroll children in school, where to find a hospital or dentist office, and how to pay our utility bills. They shielded us from the outside world until we were secure and confident enough to navigate our new environment on our own. It was during this stage when lifelong friendships were forged among the Hmong, our sponsors, neighbors, and coworkers.

The arrival to Wisconsin was a breath of fresh air for many of us despite our fear, homesickness, cultural and language barriers, and varied resettlement experiences. Wisconsin offered new opportunities for us to start our lives over again. Opportunities were there for those who desired an education and were willing to work hard. More important, for most of us, sponsors had helped ensure our basic needs were met at the outset. We had a roof over our heads, running water, a stove, and food. The majority of Hmong refugees also felt safe in their new homes. Parents and elders no longer had to listen for the sound of gunfire or worry that at any moment their homes and villages could be lost to an errant US bomb. Perhaps most significant, though, Hmong families in Wisconsin finally had a chance to take a breath and reflect on their journey to America. At the same time, they could mourn the loved ones who died during the Secret War and in the Thai refugee camps.

Upon first arriving, the Hmong tended to be very obedient and conciliatory so as not to draw any unnecessary attention. For example, we would not complain about being offered foods that we were not accustomed to. In our family we politely hid cheddar cheese blocks in a cabinet, as we did not want to be rude to our sponsors each time they brought us one. Instead of the rice staple that had sustained Hmong families for thousands of years, many sponsors gave Hmong refugee families canned foods, pasta, cheese, and milk. Thai Vue, the executive director of the La Crosse Hmong Mutual Assistance Association, puts his early encounter with the American diet this way: "For weeks, we were starving until we asked [for] and got rice."

Early on, many Hmong learned to navigate public transportation systems. Those who did not want to take a bus to work and school studied hard and earned a driver's license. Indeed, getting from place to place proved more daunting than one might think. The Hmong who could not read English or understand street signs often worried about finding their way home. To do so, people made landmarks out of what was available to them. Trees, grocery stores, department stores, gas stations, even snow, all became sign posts used by the Hmong to navigate their new surroundings. Chia Vang, an Appleton resident whose family was among the first to arrive in Wisconsin, remembers finding his way around after arriving in January. "To make sure I know how to get home, I walked on the snow instead of the sidewalk—this way I can trace my own footprints back to my house," he said.

The Hmong refugees who were able worked hard from the start to make a new and better life for themselves and their families in Wisconsin. Most Hmong parents made sure their children went to school every day. Parents worked patiently and diligently at their jobs, doing what was asked of them. Those who did not become farm laborers worked in factory jobs in paper mills, food production, and textiles. In the evenings and during the weekends, motivated parents such as my mother attended English as a Second Language (ESL) courses to learn survival English.

Those fortunate to be sponsored by well-to-do and loving sponsors were treated with compassion, dignity, and respect. They lived in warm, furnished city homes with access to hot meals and running water. But no one story can define the early Hmong resettlement experience in Wisconsin. While most sponsors tried their best to provide for Hmong refugees, I have also heard occasional stories about those who viewed their tenuous situation in a less benevolent light, as cheap and exploitable labor. Some Hmong refugees have recollected living in crowded trailers with no running water and little food to eat. Farm workers recalled doing hard manual labor for little pay, while those in factories worked long hours for minimum wage. Neng Yee Kong, a community leader and business owner in Green Bay, felt his was among the unfortunate families. Kong recalled, "[My sponsors] put me to work the next morning after I arrived. I walked while my eyes were closed, half asleep. My job was to pick up trash, empty cow poop, milk the cows, feed cows, and lift and throw hay stacks into the truck. I got yelled at a lot each time I was not able to throw hay stacks into the truck."

The Hmong in Wisconsin remained a close-knit community through the resettlement process. After some Hmong learned to drive, large groups carpooled to congregate for annual picnics or to celebrate the Hmong New Year. At these events, families often weighed the differences in their refugee experiences. Those with caring and loving sponsors were thought to be the fortunate ones, while those who were less fortunate, such as Kong, questioned why they were treated so unkindly. Gatherings such as these reinforced the Hmong's commitment to supporting one another.

Some church members recognized very early on the fragile nature of the Hmong refugee families as they tried to succeed in unfamiliar surroundings. In a few cases, church sponsors formed small committees to assist Hmong families in their struggles. These committees assisted their charges with all manner of daily life. Father Vandenberg organized different committees with specific tasks such as "housing preparation, tutoring English, teaching transportation skills, coordinating and providing child care, showing where to buy groceries, making doctor appointments, and finding jobs for the adult members."

Church committee members also recruited volunteers to protect and support the emotional well-being of Hmong refugee elders. Elders did not go into the community in the same way that younger Hmong did. They did not learn English or go to work. Instead, many elders lived in fear of being robbed, spit at, or approached by their neighbors. Most watched the outside world through a window or on television. Those who once drew a sense of self-worth from their standing in the community, one in which they were a productive cornerstone, had been stripped of their identity when forced from Laos, leaving them with little hope, faith, or apparent reason to live. Those with grandchildren to care for were more able to maintain their identity and an invaluable feeling of purpose in life.

In a few cities, volunteers offered an important sense of identity by teaching Hmong elders about Wisconsin and helping them to find their place in it. They escorted elders on field trips to botanical gardens, zoos, state parks, and government facilities such as city halls, police stations, and courthouses. While learning about their new homes, elders kept themselves busy and in better mental health. Where elders went without such assistance, depression and suicidal symptoms were common.

As refugees with legal status, Hmong families who could not find adequate work opportunities were eligible to receive Aid to Families with Dependent Children. They also qualified for food stamp vouchers. In addition, most Hmong lived in low-income housing, although such housing was more often than not located in areas where crime rates tended to be high. In Milwaukee, Hmong refugees found cheaper housing in certain blocks on the north and south sides, while in Madison, they found homes on Allied Drive, in Northport and Kennedy Heights apartment complexes, and at Bayview Community Center. All that mattered to most Hmong was to live among family and friends who supported them.

The Hmong found additional ways to be resourceful. Most Hmong mothers quickly learned the value of community resources such as the St. Vincent de Paul thrift stores. Many frequented local food pantries to fill their cupboards. Some Hmong families turned their backyards into gardens to save money and grow healthy foods. When there was no backyard to garden, some rented plots on nearby farms. They purchased large freezers to make vegetables last all year as well as to store poultry purchased from Amish farms.

The first group of Hmong refugees was still finding their way when the next wave of Hmong arrived in Wisconsin. Many settled near the Hmong clan leaders already in the region. In most cases, when a Hmong family learned where their clan leader was living, the family moved to a neighboring location in order to reestablish the community support systems central to Hmong culture in Laos.

Like so many people, Hmong parents focused their energies on raising strong and hardworking children. Parents constantly reminded their children to study hard, obey their teachers, and stay out of trouble. Hmong children were told to be patient and to ignore racial prejudice and bullying in school. Parents even instructed their children not to make too much noise to avoid attracting unwanted attention in the classroom. Children felt the pressure to behave well in school for other reasons as well. If children behaved badly or stepped out of line, that meant trouble for the whole family. Parents who missed work to take care of children sent home from school lost wages they could not afford to lose.

When children were asleep and work was done for the day, some Hmong refugee parents tossed and turned in their beds. Although they were acclimating to their new way of life in a distant land during the day, at night their thoughts returned to their villages in Laos and the camps in

Thailand. Many mourned the loss of their brothers, sisters, parents, or other relatives during the Secret War. Sleepless in Wisconsin, Hmong refugees imagined strategies of persuasion they could use to convince those who stayed behind to come to America. Some wished they could return to the camps and explain that the terrifying rumors of monsters and flesh-eating dragons and stories of wives sleeping with dogs were all false, the terrible by-products of cultural misunderstandings and rumor. When anxious minds finally slept, they dreamed of a reunion with those still on the other side of the world.

Ultimately, the honeymoon period faded away as issues with younger Hmong attracted media attention, causing misconceptions about Hmong cultural practices to spread. Reports of fighting in schools caused the mainstream population to fear their new neighbors instead of getting to know them. People would see groups of Hmong teens bonding together in support of each other and label them as gangs. Instead of building bridges, many let their fear become a barrier. Racist misconceptions filled the void, with some people accusing the Hmong of eating dog meat, not paying taxes, fraudulently using public assistance, and not learning English quickly enough. Churches and sponsors attempted to combat the rise of certain stigmas, but they could do only so much to protect vulnerable Hmong families still relatively new to America.

As I look back, I can say for certain that refugee children such as me were lucky to come to Wisconsin. While my parents were afraid and reluctant to settle so far from Southeast Asia, I know they made the right choice when they left Ban Vinai for America. Although many Hmong families found themselves living in areas where crime was prevalent and where good employment was scarce, we were fortunate. We felt and knew for certain that we had found a safe haven in Wisconsin, a place we could finally call home.

## COMMUNITY LEADERSHIP

Traditionally, the Hmong have a strong sense of community in which everyone has a responsibility to ensure their actions benefit the whole. Individual actions benefit or harm everyone alike, so the Hmong encourage and value selflessness and generosity. Men and women, old and young, all have a responsibility to their family and neighbors. Each person has a role to play, determined in part by birth, gender, kinship, and age. Elders, considered wise and rich in life experiences, command the most respect. Children are learners until they marry and start a family. Mothers teach, preserve cultural traditions, and generally manage domestic affairs. In addition to sharing these roles, fathers are traditionally considered leaders—of their families, clans, and communities. As the Hmong have adjusted to life in their new homes, some of the traditional roles have evolved.

My father, NhaiPao Vue, was a clan leader. When the Hmong first arrived in Wisconsin, clan leaders such as my father, as well as former military leaders, saw it as their job to establish a new, informal support system into which the Hmong could bring their families. They formed formal alliances by means of nonprofit and cooperative agencies that served Hmong communities. Clan leaders often rotated through the governing boards of these agencies.

As the Hmong continued to arrive in the unfamiliar environment and culture of Wisconsin over a period of years, clan and former military leaders searched for and formed their own support system within their communities to network and to address their homesickness in Wisconsin. The few Hmong leaders who spoke some English became interpreters and traveled hours away to interpret and give a basic orientation for a new arriving Hmong family. This orientation was critical as the new family needed to know how to turn on the stove and faucet in the bathroom, flush the toilet, use a refrigerator and a freezer, where to buy groceries, and who to call during an emergency. Those who learned how to drive arranged car pools and sometimes drove two to three hours across the state to network and build connections in other communities. Gathering places rotated between the Fox Cities, Wausau, and Eau Claire. Eventually, annual picnics and celebrations of the Hmong New Year became part of the routine. The events were opportunities to give thanks for a new life and to exchange valuable knowledge and resources. Boys and girls wore colorful clothes, handmade decorative jewelry, and jingled coin purses as reminders of the hard work and sacrifices of many.

Despite the best efforts of those such as Father Vandenberg and the many able volunteers who gave their time to assist Hmong refugees, local churches, resettlement agencies, and state government offices were overwhelmed when it came to providing adequate aid to the Hmong. They simply had no way to overcome the cultural and language barriers between the Hmong and Americans while simultaneously meeting the growing legal, educational, and health needs of every Hmong family. Thus, Hmong clan leaders and veterans took it upon themselves to alleviate the many daily stresses within Hmong communities, from acquiring food to facilitating access to education to providing financial assistance for funerals. They arranged carpools to Asian grocery stores for families lacking transportation and created funeral funds to help families pay for traditional Hmong funerals. Overwhelmed with their communities' needs, clan leaders soon put in place the infrastructure needed to support their homes and communities.

Their efforts resulted in the formation of a new statewide agency, the Hmong Mutual Assistance Association of Wisconsin (HMAAW). Founded in 1978 and incorporated in 1980, the HMAAW was first led by Colonel Yong Chue Yang, a veteran of Vang Pao's Special Guerilla Unit active during the war. The HMAAW served Hmong populations in Appleton, Green Bay, Eau Claire, La Crosse, Madison, Manitowoc, Milwaukee, Sheboygan, and Wausau.

At first, the HMAAW relied on volunteers and donations to manage its operations. In 1982, that changed when the HMAAW received thirty-five thousand dollars in federal pass-through funds from the Office of Refugee Resettlement. Its work as a statewide entity was sufficient in the early years of Hmong resettlement, but the number of arrivals increased significantly by 1980, creating a need for more local assistance. Beginning that year, Hmong Mutual Assistance Associations (MAAs) began opening in counties throughout Wisconsin, including Sheboygan, Outagamie, Brown, Milwaukee, Dane, Manitowoc, Eau Claire, La Crosse, Marathon, and elsewhere. The MAAs were created to provide immediate assistance, with the ultimate goal of helping each community's Hmong residents become self-reliant. They worked closely with the State Refugee Office, which was created in 1980 to address the needs of

Southeast Asian refugees arriving in Wisconsin. From the start, MAAs worked to find employment and provide social and transportation services for the Hmong people of Wisconsin. Members of MAAs were not trained as grassroots advocates, nor did they specialize in creating or implementing political or educational policies, but they often served as the Hmong community's main contact with the media and government officials. In addition to these services, MAAs often arranged celebrations of the Hmong New Year and became important community gathering spaces.

Failure and challenges preceded success. The bilingual Hmong staff, working more than eight hours a day for little or no pay, often felt burned out. Employees lacked the resources and support to apply for and win essential funding. At the same time, Hmong MAAs competed with other local agencies for precious resources. Finally, when offering assistance, MAAs had to be sensitive to the Hmong's intricate clan-based webs of leadership. The strength of the bonds created through blood and marriage could make it difficult for an outside agency to get involved.

Hmong MAAs grew rapidly to aid Hmong refugees. There remained a need, however, for a larger organization to oversee and administer local Hmong MAAs. Therefore, in 1996, an umbrella agency, the Wisconsin United Coalition of Mutual Assistance Association (WUCMAA), took over. Xia Vue Yang served as the first board president. The WUCMAA brought MAA board presidents and directors together to meet and improve the services available to their communities. WUCMAA offered the additional benefit of reducing the workload of the Wisconsin State Refugee Office, which could now communicate with one agency rather than fifteen. The MAAs became bridges between the Hmong and mainstream community in Wisconsin. Refugee and nonrefugee agencies, officials, and the media contacted the MAAs when issues in Hmong communities caught the attention of those on the outside.

While Hmong MAAs worked diligently on behalf of Hmong refugees in Wisconsin, Hmong leaders in other states searched for solutions to a problem that Hmong in states such as Minnesota and California also faced. A national conversation began that asked how Hmong people everywhere could reduce their dependency on public welfare. Maly Yang, Chasong Yang, and Ying Ly, all Hmong MAA leaders from Wisconsin, participated in a national effort spearheaded by Toyo Biddle, a staff member at the federal Office of Refugee Resettlement, and Tony

Vang, the director of the Lao Family Community of Fresno organization in California. In 1987, at a conference in Atlanta, Georgia, attendees created the Hmong American National Development (HAND) subcommittee, a body committed to studying and fixing the problem of Hmong welfare dependency in America. Five years later, HAND incorporated a national nonprofit organization, Hmong National Development, to provide support and resources to local MAAs. Hmong leadership at the local and national levels played an important role in moving Hmong refugees toward economic self-sufficiency. Their hard work paid off almost immediately, as 426 Hmong families went off public assistance in 1992, and another 270 families required fewer welfare dollars, according to the ORR's annual report to Congress in 1993. The Hmong welfare dependency in Wisconsin rate fell from 87 percent in 1989 to 4 percent in 2010. The services of the MAAs helped move more Hmong into the workforce in the early years, building a foundation for young Hmong growing up in America to attain increasing levels of education and success.

MAAs also fielded grievances from some Hmong when changes to welfare policy brought on negative consequences. The 1996 passage of the national Personal Responsibility and Work Opportunity Reconciliation Act, which made refugees ineligible for public assistance for five years, was met with anger and disappointment from Hmong veterans throughout Wisconsin. Hmong MAAs and their leaders were pillars of support during this sensitive time and fought to restore benefits for Hmong veterans who held legal status.

In Milwaukee, where the highest concentration of Hmong refugees in Wisconsin had settled, the first Hmong charter school, the Hmong American Peace Academy (HAPA), was established in 2000 with MAA involvement. Still in operation, the mission of the school is to improve elementary education for Hmong children while preserving cultural heritage. In addition, the La Crosse MAA and clan leaders raised enough capital to renovate an old building that was later named the Hmong Culture and Community Center of La Crosse. It opened in 2005 as a communal gathering place and a venue to house Hmong funeral services.

Local leaders also looked for help within the ranks of the military officials who had led them to America, particularly General Vang Pao. In 1977, according to Chia Vang of Appleton, community leaders such as Youa True Vang collected donations to fly Vang Pao to Wisconsin from his residences in Montana and California multiple times. Regional meetings were arranged at which the general would speak to the Hmong about adjusting to life in Wisconsin. The general encouraged those in the audience to work together as a community. The motivational speech proved effective, as plans were laid right away for improvement. Some Hmong began to thrive economically as family members and relatives pooled resources to start their own businesses, first mom-and-pop ethnic grocery stores and later video stores and restaurants. A local grocery store, the Community Food Market, opened in Appleton. The co-op sold the same foods available at the Asian grocery store in Green Bay, thereby saving Appleton residents time and money. The first Asian video store in Appleton was founded in 1984. In the early 1990s, the Vang brothers and their families founded the Chengpeng Restaurant on College Avenue in Appleton. Mekong Fresh Meat, named for the Mekong River in Laos, started serving meat to a mostly Hmong clientele in the Mosinee area in 1993 and still employs many recent arrivals with limited English. And in 1995, Asian-American Wholesale opened for business in Milwaukee. Other Hmong businesses include insurance agencies and beauty salons.

Many of these success stories came about with the support of community leaders who made it their mission to rebuild what the Hmong had lost and, in the process, become productive citizens alongside their neighbors. Hmong community leaders rise to the occasion in times of crisis! It must be said, too, that clan leaders such as my father would not have succeeded without support from churches and local and state governments. Through bringing these different entities together to assist the Hmong, MAAs demonstrate what can be accomplished in Wisconsin when people from different backgrounds work together. Some attempts to enable the Hmong to be self-sufficient had mixed results. The MAAs partnered with the State Refugee Office on the Key State Initiative, an employment program that tried to put all able-bodied members of a family to work. Although the program succeeded in removing many Hmong families from public assistance and helping them find jobs, many of these families became the working poor, continuing to struggle financially.

MAAs and the community leaders who built them are dying out. Most Hmong no longer qualify for the refugee funding needed to fund their daily operating costs, as federal money is becoming harder to come by. What will become of them is a question urgently in need of an answer.

✖✖

## SUCCESS AND STRUGGLES

The Hmong Mutual Assistance Associations established in the early 1980s have played a central part in reducing Hmong welfare dependency in Wisconsin, but their success has brought instability to the many branches. As the number of Hmong welfare recipients falls and as the Hmong refugee resettlement rate in Wisconsin slows, federal funding for MAAs has declined proportionally. Although low-income Hmong households are still in need, the remaining Hmong MAAs are struggling to provide adequate care to those they serve.

Overall, however, the story of Hmong MAAs in Wisconsin is one of triumph over adversity. In collaboration with the Key State Initiative program that promoted the entry of secondary wage earners into the workforce, MAAs made it possible for any willing Hmong adult—male or female—to land a job. The majority of Hmong refugees were placed in low-wage blue-collar jobs, including entry-level positions at food-processing or meat-packaging plants, as well as on assembly lines in paper mills. Because Hmong families tend to be large, every able family member needed to do his or her part.

As Hmong household incomes increased, so too did their ability to purchase homes and businesses. Although it was still difficult for a single Hmong family to afford a home or open a business, multiple Hmong families found ways to secure financing for loans by pooling their savings. At the same time, Hmong MAAs made the same transition from tenant to owner, as Hmong MAAs purchased their own office space in Wausau and Appleton in 1997.

By the mid-2000s, funding for Hmong MAAs began to dwindle. Although Hmong communities in Wisconsin still required the same financial, legal, and health services provided by Hmong MAAs for decades, the Hmong had been in the United States long enough that they were losing their refugee status and, with it, access to federal funding. Budget cuts also were likely due to a national economic downturn. Although the State Refugee Office repeatedly warned Hmong MAAs that federal funding cuts were probably unavoidable, the organizations were unable to do enough to diversify their revenue streams. The loss of federal dollars was a rude awakening for leadership and staff, some of whom were inexperienced at running a nonprofit organization, developing employees, or securing funding.

## CULTURAL CLASHES

In 1975, many lifelong residents of places such as Wausau, Appleton, and Green Bay had never seen anything like the Hmong refugees in their small cities, which were and remain predominantly white. They recognized men, women, and children like the Hmong from the footage of the Vietnam War they saw on television, but it is likely that most of them knew very little, if anything at all, about Laos, the Secret War, or why the Hmong had suddenly appeared on the doorstep of their lives.

The Hmong carried with them to Wisconsin a culture rich with traditional values and practices. From Laos, the Hmong brought a kinship network organized through patrilineal clan systems in which elders command respect. They kept alive ancient practices to keep their bodies and souls healthy, including shamanism, *hu plig* (soul calling), *kav* (coining), and *khawv koob* (magic healing). Traditional herbs remained in use as medicine and flavors for food. The vibrancy of Hmong music and artwork could be heard and seen in Hmong homes and at craft markets. Birth, marriage, and death were all celebrated in the manner Hmong had known for generations. In some cases, these major events were attended to according to the Christian customs some Hmong adopted. Regardless of these deviations, though, a sense of community and connection persisted among the Hmong who began their lives anew in Wisconsin. As Yang Dao wrote in *Hmong at the Turning Point*, those who "descended from a common ancestor live together insofar as possible [to] form a community of interests."

Hmong cultural and traditional practices can be parsed into three major categories: birth, marriage, and death. Within each category, traditional rites call for certain things. For instance, a chicken, pig, or cow is ritually sacrificed at times. *Hu plig* is a "soul calling" ceremony done to call home a soul that is believed to be lost, such as in the case of a sick person who has lost his or her appetite for food and become frail or a refugee believed to have lost his or her soul on the trip from Laos to the

United States. Wedding, funeral, and other cultural traditions can involve butchering a chicken or sacrificing a cow or pig. These rituals were performed respectfully and humanely, using animals commonly slaughtered for food in the United States, but non-Hmong community members objected to the practice. Upon their arrival, the Hmong had no knowledge of any city ordinances that prevented the possession or slaughter of livestock on their property. When neighbors reported these rituals, it was difficult for the police to explain to the Hmong what they had done wrong, just as it was hard for the Hmong to communicate that they believed they had the right to practice their culture. In the end, Hmong leaders such as my father had to find new ways to practice their ceremonies. For example, a shaman would prepare a pig for killing in the ritual way, after which the pig was returned to a slaughterhouse.

Other aspects of Hmong funerals have also attracted unwanted negative attention, beginning the 1980s and continuing into the twenty-first century. Traditional Hmong funerals can last up to three days depending on the age of the deceased, featuring a twenty-four-hour hum of activity, making it difficult to host at a funeral parlor. The high volume of visitors from near and far frequently can result in parked vehicles overflowing into the surrounding streets, causing neighbors to complain. Such complaints and difficulties led many funeral homes to discontinue such services to the Hmong, who have had to piece together other solutions. A few Hmong families who own enough land hold funerals on their farms, if there is enough room to do so, or modify their traditions to meet the policies and requirements of funeral homes. In some larger communities such as Milwaukee, Hmong entrepreneurs have founded funeral homes to specifically cater to the Hmong. In La Crosse, the MAA raised funds to build and run the Hmong Culture and Community Center, which includes space for funerals. In many locations, however, Hmong families have continued to experience the frustration of not being able to provide elaborate and lengthy funerals to properly return deceased loved ones to their birthplaces and reunite them with ancestors.

The tension between Hmong and Americans was enough to cause some Hmong to leave their communities, seeking relocation to other cities or even states as the easiest option open to them. If Hmong people were being harassed by their American neighbors, they seldom called the police to resolve disputes. Many Hmong did not understand the unfamiliar American legal system and feared the police.

Such fears had the undesirable consequence of fueling rumors powerful enough to sway decisions made half a world away in Thailand. Many Hmong men and women believed terrible stories about life in the United States, stories that gave them cause to wait for a return to Laos that would never happen. According to one particularly grotesque rumor, Hmong wives were forced to sleep with dogs owned by their sponsors. Some Hmong were even convinced they would be sacrificed to a monster if they came to America, imagining something similar to the famous scene in *King Kong* in which a human sacrifice is offered to the giant ape. Imagine the fear that took hold, then, when a Hmong family in America encountered certain US traditions for the first time. One Hmong man whom I interviewed related that when he was newly arrived to Wisconsin, he opened his door after hearing the doorbell ring and saw the face of King Kong staring back at him. The masked figure asked him a question in a language he could not understand: "Trick or treat?" Such innocent misunderstandings precipitated the spread of misinformation, reinforcing what some Hmong believed to be legitimate reasons to stay away from the United States.

Breakdowns in the lines of communication and cultural differences between the Hmong community and the outside led to even more unfortunate or even tragic misunderstandings. In the early 1980s, a Wisconsin teacher noticed dark purple bruises on the body of a student. The teacher notified a social worker, who then phoned the police. The teacher mistakenly believed the child had been physically abused. In reality, the welts were a result of "coining," a practice in which a coin is used to rub the skin as a cure for ailments such as stomachaches and headaches. The clan leader was arrested in front of his family on charges of abuse. Embarrassed and ashamed, he hanged himself, perhaps not understanding that the US justice system would afford him a trial and a chance for his name to be cleared. When a person is put in handcuffs in Laos, it means they are guilty and will be sentenced to prison.

❧✺

## ART AND CUISINE

Although some Hmong traditions attracted negative public attention, other aspects of Hmong culture were seen in a more positive light by sympathetic onlookers and have since found a niche in Wisconsin. Hmong cuisine, with its many fragrant and flavorful herbs such as lemongrass, cilantro, mint, and ginger, has drawn notice for its taste and health benefits. Our parents brought Hmong foods to school potlucks, where Hmong eggrolls quickly became a hit. The ins and outs of Hmong cooking are passed down from generation to generation. My mother, Xia Vang, taught me to embrace a Hmong traditional diet, and I taught my children the same. It is important to maintain a thriving Hmong food culture, as food is medicine to the Hmong. It is more than just something we eat. According to Dia Cha of St. Cloud State University in Minnesota, the Hmong use herbs in their cooking not only to enhance the flavor of many dishes but also to provide health benefits. Cilantro, for example, has antibacterial properties, and lemongrass promotes circulation and can be used to decrease swelling, Dia Cha said.

The artistry and beauty of Hmong music and craftwork have also amassed widespread admiration. The *qeej*, a six-reed bamboo instrument, can be heard at Hmong New Year celebrations and summer festivals. Its music also is traditionally used in funerals to pronounce someone's death and accompany the soul to find its ancestors, as well as in wedding ceremonies to send a family member off into a new life. Hmong embroidery, which we call "story cloth," and reverse applique are fixtures at quilting shows and craft and flea markets. Mao Yang of Watertown and Joua Lor of Madison have sold their art at the farmers' market on the Capitol Square in Madison and during the annual Maxwell Street Days festival. In the Fox Cities, Sheng Vang of Milwaukee and Moua Lee of Sheboygan have sold beautiful Hmong art at Octoberfest in Appleton and at other local art shows and flea markets.

The Hmong artwork that gained acclaim was developed at the refugee camps in Thailand to record what the Hmong were going through and to provide a therapeutic outlet while being confined in refugee camps. Traditionally, Hmong artwork was made for ritualistic uses, such as for funeral clothing or to wear when courting at the New Year festival. That changed when Hmong men and women at the camp in Ban Vinai found themselves with extra time on their hands. Stitched in softer and paler colors than traditional Hmong craftwork, the *paj ntaub*, or story cloth, is a narrative first and work of art second. The *paj ntaub* is a visual historical record, a register of the Secret War and a time of rapid change and diaspora in Hmong culture. When the Hmong came to America, they found a market for story cloths. Money earned from their sale was often mailed to family members still in the Thai camps. Professional artists eventually took notice of the *paj ntaub*, and in 1985, the Kohler Art Center in Sheboygan showcased a *paj ntaub* exhibit.

As time goes by, fewer Hmong have the knowledge and skills to animate certain traditions of Hmong culture. As elders age and pass away, their talents and abilities are lost. For many years, only one herbalist Hmong woman, for example, lived in Madison, and since her death, no one has carried on the traditional practices of *muab tshuaj ntsuab* (herbalism). Modern healthcare is more attractive than traditional healing practices to younger Hmong. Celebrations of the Hmong New Year are also less common than they once were; *kwv txhiaj* (poetry songs) are rarely taught and sung, and some musical instruments are played less frequently. These include the *raj* (flute), *ncas* (jaw harp), and *nkauj laug ncas* (two-string violin). In the same vein, *mej koob* (marriage negotiators) do not sing wedding songs in the way they once did.

Cultural traditions are woven into the fabric of the Hmong community. Without them, the ties that bind the Hmong together might weaken and fray. As the first generation of Hmong refugees grows older and dies, it is uncertain what will happen to Hmong traditions and culture in the years ahead. Will Christianity become the dominant faith in the Hmong community? Will the knowledge of the herbalists and shamans be lost? These important questions will be answered by the youngest generation of Hmong in Wisconsin who are nearing a turning point in Hmong history.

Children in the Ban Vinai camp in Thailand pose for a photo in May 1976, just before one of the boys was sent to live with his uncle in France. Separation of family members was common at the time as Hmong refugees living in camps waited to be resettled elsewhere. The rest of the children pictured were later resettled in Wisconsin and Minnesota. Pictured are Mytia Ly, Phia Vue, Thaivone Ly, Sida Ly, Mai Zong Vue, Tou Lee Vue, and Long Vue.

A refugee in the Wat Thomkrabok camp sews a cloth in 1995. Hmong refugees living in Thai camps would send their work to relatives who had resettled in other countries, and the relatives would sell the goods and send the money back. The sewing served both economic and therapeutic purposes, helping to keep refugees' minds busy and to provide funds to feed their families.

Neng Thao (seated, center), who reunited with her son NhaiPao Vue after thirteen years of separation following the fall of Saigon in 1975, is pictured with several generations of family in Appleton, Wisconsin, in 1989.

Yong Kay Moua with his wife, Houa Vue, and their daughter, Mary ak Kashia, in front of their house in Eau Claire in 1979.

Yong Kay Moua

In the 1980s, in the early years after Hmong refugees arrived in Wisconsin, sports were mostly played by Hmong boys, but a few Hmong girls paved the way, starting with volleyball. By the early 1990s, Hmong female teams such as the one in this photo participated in Hmong festivals on Memorial Day and Labor Day.

It is typical for Hmong families, especially mothers and daughters or fathers and sons, to take photos together each time they visit one another. The frequent separation of family members during refugee relocation has caused the Hmong to appreciate one another's company even more when they have opportunities to gather.

A group of boys from Madison in traditional costumes at a Hmong New Year celebration in the 1990s.

Mao Thao, a Hmong artist who lives in Watertown, sells story cloths and crafts at Maxwell Street Days on State Street in Madison in 1997. The creation of Hmong story cloths not only provided economic and therapeutic benefits to Hmong refugees, but also recorded the Hmong history from China, to Laos, to Thailand, and finally to America.

In a traditional Hmong wedding, the bride is introduced to the groom's side of the family. This ritual varies from family to family but in general includes a soul calling ceremony (*hu plig*), after which relatives will tie white strings on the bride and groom's hands and wish them a healthy and prosperous marriage with many children.

A Hmong girl was included in a ritual at an event to congratulate her mother on a career achievement. *Hu plig*, or soul calling, is a traditional Hmong healing ritual used on many occasions such as adding a new member to the family through birth or marriage, healing sickness, and celebrating the Hmong New Year. In Laos, Hmong adopted *khi tes*, or the practice of string tying, from the Laotians and added this to the *hu plig*.

A typical Hmong feast at a Milwaukee home in the early 2000s. The Hmong enjoy such feasts at celebrations such as weddings or graduations. The Hmong have a saying that applies on such occasions, "*Tsev ti los neeg tsis ti*," or "The house may be tight, but the heart is abundant."

## THE CHANGING ROLES OF WOMEN

It is a blessing and a curse to be born a girl in the Hmong community. When a child is born, the first question that family members and relatives ask is, *Tus me ab yog tus mus ev dej los tus ev taws?* ("Is the baby the one to get water or wood for fire?"). In other words, is it a girl or a boy? Gender roles are clearly defined in traditional Hmong culture. Girls are taught to do domestic chores, and boys are raised to work outside the home. But Hmong culture has never been monolithic or static, and so unsurprisingly, gender roles changed when the Hmong left Laos. In the United States, where a new environment and challenges awaited, they modified and stretched their cultural boundaries to incorporate the needs of their time and place. I am a living example of change in action.

Generally, women moved on from life in Laos more quickly than men did. As war veterans, many Hmong men were still recovering from their wartime losses and experiences, and most women had no choice but to anchor the family affairs. They had no time to grieve their losses or be ashamed of their broken English and so learned the language more quickly than many men. The once clear lines that separated men's work from women's work blurred rapidly as a result. Hmong women went to school, worked outside the home, and assumed leadership roles in families and the community. Women of different ages immediately found themselves driving, shopping for groceries, banking, and working to support their families financially.

Hmong women, educated and uneducated alike, pushed through many difficulties and became leaders in their communities. Youa Lor, known as Mrs. Tou Her in the Hmong community, performed admirable services for the Hmong in Wausau and throughout the state. She was instrumental in organizing and developing the Hmong Mutual Assistance Association of Wisconsin (HMAAW), of which she was a board officer. Her took meetings with public officials to field their questions, iron out grievances, and lobby for an expansion of refugee services. Her even attracted national media coverage. The *Atlantic Monthly* ran a story in its April 1994 issue called "The Ordeal of Immigration in Wausau," wherein the efforts of Youa Her are given proper credit. The article referred to Her as "an educated, articulate leader of the early wave of Hmong settlers."

Like Her, Houa V. Moua stepped up to help her community in its time of need. Based in Eau Claire, Moua made a quick study of English. She served others as an interpreter and community liaison while also finding time to be a wife and mother. In doing so, however, Moua exposed herself and her husband to criticism from some members of the Hmong community who were unnerved by her atypical behavior. But women like Her and Moua did not have time to worry about what such people thought. If children needed to be driven to school or if relatives had important appointments, and a woman learned enough English to get a driver's license before her husband did, it made sense for her to take them.

With no formal training or certifications, Hmong men sometimes had a difficult time earning enough money to support their families. The average Hmong household in the late 1970s and early 1980s had six children, so a father needed more than low-wage work to provide for his family. The Key State Initiative, a federal program for refugees piloted in Wisconsin and a few other states, stepped in and encouraged Hmong women to enter the workforce. As secondary wage earners, some Hmong women found low-paying jobs at manufacturing companies. They sewed, cleaned, or worked on assembly lines. Such decisions sometimes led to familial conflict. When a Hmong woman made the decision to go to work, she did not always find the support she needed from her husband or family and friends. Although they took great pride in their ability to provide for their families, some women felt guilty that they could not stay home to care for their children. Problems at home surfaced, for example, when a husband and a wife worked different shifts, leading to breakdowns in communication and questions about who would watch the children. Generally speaking, trust eroded in many marriages, and rumors of extramarital affairs flew when both parents worked. Tragically, at least one such rumor led to violence. In 1990, Yee Yang of Eau Claire was murdered by her husband, allegedly for having an affair.

Despite the hardships that many Hmong refugee women endured, they remained determined to find success in the workforce. Many benefited from the Wisconsin Refugee Women's Initiative, a social services program geared toward solving domestic disputes. The program sponsored regional and statewide prevention workshops and conferences that introduced attendees to certain aspects of the American legal code and offered helpful ways to manage stress, promote conflict resolution in the home, and foster strong networks of emotional support. Many of the Hmong refugee women who participated emerged as leading voices in their neighborhoods. When the Hmong American Women's Association opened in Milwaukee in 1993, its founders, Mayvue Lor, Joua V. Moua, Mayhoua Moua, and Nor Yang, withstood criticisms of their work from their own communities in order to lend a hand to the Hmong women who needed it most. A few years later, Mary Xiong and others established a Hmong women's organization in Green Bay. It is telling that the women who made the biggest difference in their communities had encouragement from their spouses. Without anyone at home to spur them on, it is likely that some of these influential Hmong women would have given in to the intense pressures on them to stay in the traditional domestic role Hmong women had known in Laos.

The same group of emboldened Hmong women who defied tradition when they came to Wisconsin urged their daughters to avoid marrying young and to attend high school and, in some cases, college. They wanted their daughters to have the same career opportunities as other American women. Before the Secret War, Hmong women used to marry as early as fourteen in Laos, meaning they started families and kept households before most American girls had graduated middle school. PaFoua Yang's mother had the courage to call off her daughter's marriage to a Hmong man in Texas when the girl was in high school. The mother and daughter paid a terrible emotional price to do it, but they gained more than they lost. In 1995, Yang became the first Hmong female doctor in America. Like Yang's mother, my mother and my older sister risked their reputations and subjected themselves to criticism when they supported my decision to attend college and start a career before I married. Other Hmong women who ended up in Wisconsin have accomplished great things. Kaying Xiong became the first female Hmong principal in the United States. Mee Moua resettled from Laos to Wisconsin and became the first person of Hmong descent to hold a state senate seat in the United States when she was elected to the Minnesota Senate. Der Lyfoung was the first Hmong woman to work for the state of Wisconsin. Others include Bo Thao, the first Hmong female executive director at Hmong National Development, Inc.; Chris Her-Xiong, CEO of Hmong American Peace Academy; Miva Yang, the first Hmong nurse in Wisconsin; Mor Yang, the first female Hmong school counselor;

Maly Yang, the first female Hmong social worker; and Pahoua Yang, the first female Hmong psychologist in a management position as the vice president of the Mental Health Center at Wilder Foundation.

The Hmong refugee women who arrived in the first wave to Wisconsin might have struggled to picture the women some of them would become. Nor would they have been able to imagine the remarkable things their daughters would do. Hmong gender norms have changed dramatically in the four decades that have passed since the Hmong left Laos for Thailand and Thailand for America. Hmong women have learned English, started successful careers, and struck new balances between their lives in and out of the home. Many Hmong women have gained the type of respect from Hmong men and community members once denied to them. Daughters of the first wave are leaders and mothers today. They are lawyers, school principals, teachers, business owners, artists, bankers, real estate agents, social workers, doctors, politicians, and university professors. They are leaving legacies of positive change and accomplishment in Wisconsin for their daughters to inherit, a legacy that includes changing how Hmong people are perceived locally, statewide, and nationally. As a Hmong woman, I feel honored to be part of this ongoing process.

## CIVIL RIGHTS AND RACISM

The Hmong have always been resourceful and resilient. When they have found themselves in a new land, the Hmong have adapted their ways to their new surroundings and attempted to live on amicable terms with those nearest to them. The Hmong even have an old saying: *Nyob luag ntuj xyoog luag txuj; nyob luag teb xyoog luag ci* ("Live in a stranger's world, adopt a stranger's law; live in a stranger's land, adopt a stranger's education"). The phrase has been uttered in my house as a reminder to be patient and tolerant with others. It is often accompanied by a second pearl of wisdom, *Uv kom dhau, uv xwb yeej tsis tuag* ("Tolerate it; tolerating is not going to kill you").

The Hmong held fast to these beliefs even when they were victims of severe racial prejudice and discrimination. In the early 1980s, Hmong confronted abuses of every kind when they arrived in Wisconsin. Hmong were subjected to verbal, emotional, and physical harm. Individuals, groups, and entire communities were targeted. Elders and parents kept to their maxims, tolerating incidents as they came with patience and fortitude. For nearly a decade, Hmong refugees often responded to racism and intolerance by keeping quiet and sweeping racial tensions under the rug.

When incidents escalated to the degree that they became unbearable, racism was reported to family and clan leaders. A few Hmong communities began to discuss what they were experiencing as a group, sharing information with sponsors and at community gatherings. For example, at the Hmong Women's Motivational Workshop held in La Crosse in 1991, nineteen Hmong women shared types of racism they had experienced. The women reported being yelled at and attacked physically. They were assaulted with derogatory language and taunts that they should "go back to their country."

Well-meaning sponsors often advised the Hmong to keep a low profile when it came to dealing with racism. In their minds and in the opinion of many Hmong elders, ignoring incidents was the best way to prevent an escalation to violence. That strategy worked for individuals but was less effective in dealing with the kinds of systemic racism that impacted the Hmong community at large. Problems such as those brought to light by the Hmong women at the meeting in La Crosse were simply too ubiquitous and too visible to ignore.

An incident that occurred in 1981 speaks to the ways in which popular misconceptions often fueled racism against the Hmong. That year, white students in Eau Claire hit Joe Bee Xiong, a Hmong student at Memorial High School. His assailants accused Xiong of eating dog meat. Hmong community leaders, the Eau Claire police, and members of the media all took notice, and a coordinated effort to educate the public about the Hmong followed. Rumors that the Hmong ate dog meat were dispelled, and information was supplied to the people of Eau Claire to help them understand why the Hmong had come to Wisconsin as refugees. Shortly after the incident involving Xiong, two clan leaders, Vam Sawm Xyooj and Paj Tsab Xyooj, moved their families and clans out of Wisconsin. They did not believe that the Hmong would be accepted in the Eau Claire community or anywhere in Wisconsin. Vam Sawm Xyooj took his clan to North Carolina, and Paj Tsab Xyooj moved his clan to California.

While some Hmong men preferred to dodge confrontation, some Hmong women tended to denounce racism as they met it, seeing incidents of racism as opportunities to educate misguided people who knew little about the Hmong. Houa Moua, a bilingual interpreter with the Eau Claire Public Health Department, is an example of a Hmong woman fighting bigotry with education. One day, Houa and a Hmong coworker were taking a break outside and chatting in Hmong. A white teenager walked by and made unpleasant remarks toward them. When the teenager yelled, "Cheng, go home," using a slur word usually directed at Chinese immigrants, Moua informed him she could not because, "It is not 5 o'clock yet!" When the teenager replied, "You should speak English every day so you can move out of public housing," Moua and her coworker informed him that they did work and did not qualify for public assistance. "We worked hard in the Vietnam War. You should welcome us!" she told him.

That teenager made the remarks he did to Moua because he mistakenly believed that all Hmong are on public assistance. Nevertheless, that stereotype and others like it have unfairly been held as strikes against the Hmong. Other pervasive stereotypes include the idea that the Hmong do not pay taxes but drive late-model vans. Although it is true that many Hmong were once on public assistance or lived in public housing when they first arrived in the country, is it also true that employed Hmong pay their federal and state taxes. As for driving new vans, the Hmong need reliable transportation to get many people to work, school, and appointments. It used to be common for ten to fifteen families to pool their money to buy a reliable van.

Over time, clan leaders, elders, and parents had more to worry about than racism. Crime, something impossible to divorce entirely from racism and its effects, gradually became an issue in Hmong communities. Police became increasingly aware of the Hmong when Hmong got into traffic accidents or were involved in cases of domestic abuse. Incidents where the welfare of children was called into question also occurred.

Crime became a more serious issue as the Hmong who came to America as children and young teens grew older. This group, who might not remember their home country but are not fully accepted in their adopted country either, is known as the "1.5 generation." Unlike their parents and grandparents, members of the 1.5 generation have been less willing to turn a blind eye toward the prejudice that negatively affects themselves and their families. They knew about and felt the scars that racial prejudice had left on the hearts of their parents and elders— and they wanted to do something about it. Driven to take action, the 1.5-generation Hmong have stood up to racial slurs, often by speaking out against the injustices they have witnessed firsthand. Some became community organizers who taught their parents about civil rights.

Sometimes, when words were not enough, they have fought back with their fists. Chong Lee Her, now a social worker in Eau Claire, said that fighting was the only thing that made racial harassment stop when he was growing up. For two years, Her ignored racial taunts, turning away when students swore or spit at him. He joined the track and wrestling teams, hoping to earn respect, but still other students tormented him. "The time I gained some of the students' respect was when I knocked down a huge guy—the biggest guy and the leader of the wrestling group—after school outside in the playground," Her said in an interview in 2011. "A large crowd of students were watching us fight. After that, they left me alone."

In the 2000s, violent and nonviolent racial tensions between whites and Hmong brought more regional and national attention to the ongoing realities of racial inequality and racial violence still alive in Hmong communities. Chai Soua Vang was deer hunting in northwest Wisconsin in 2004 when he was confronted by a group of white hunters who asked him to leave their property. Reports allege that the white hunters directed racial slurs at Vang and that an argument ensued. Vang contends that one of the hunters, Terry Willers, then fired at him. Fearing for his life, Vang returned fire in what he argued was self-defense. When the shooting stopped, five of the white hunters were dead and three were wounded. One of the wounded later died. Nearly a year later, Chai Soua Vang was convicted by an all-white jury on six counts of first-degree intentional homicide and three charges of attempted homicide. He was sentenced to life in prison without parole. Covered widely in the national media, the case served as an unfortunate introduction for many Americans who had not been exposed to the Hmong community before. For those who looked closer, it also raised questions about the toll that repeated experiences of racism can take on a community and on the role that race plays in the justice system. Lu Lippold and Mark Tang, who directed a documentary about the case, said in an interview with NPR that a more diverse jury might have reached a different conclusion. They also noted the frustration in the Hmong community that incidents of racial bullying frequently experienced by Hmong hunters did not come up in the trial.

Another hunting tragedy occurred in January 2007. Cha Vang, a thirty-year-old Hmong man from Green Bay, was hunting squirrels in the Peshtigo Harbor Wildlife Area when he got into an altercation with James Nichols, a white hunter from Peshtigo. Nichols shot and stabbed Vang and hid the corpse in the woods. Hmong of the 1.5 generation were upset that it took too long for the Marinette County district attorney to file charges against Nichols and that the case was not being prosecuted as a hate crime in spite of evidence that Nichols had made racist statements about the Hmong. Hmong advocates from St. Paul sat in the courtroom throughout the Nichols trial. They were there to observe the legal process and to do what they could to prevent an unjust ruling similar to the one they believe was handed down in the case against Chai Vang. Nichols pleaded self-defense, but in October 2007, a jury convicted him on the charge of second-degree intentional homicide. The ruling upset many in the Hmong community who were hoping Nichols would be found guilty of first-degree murder.

The murder of Cha Vang prompted many Hmong youth and young professionals to speak out against hate crimes. Hmong youth from Minnesota and Wisconsin joined Hmong MAAs to get involved in the community. Together they held candlelight vigils to honor Cha Vang and organized a protest rally at the state capitol. In January, shortly after Cha Vang was murdered, leaders of the Hmong 1.5 generation held a town hall meeting at a hotel in Green Bay. More than five hundred concerned Hmong were in the crowd. For the first time in Wisconsin, Hmong refugees' perspectives and voices had an audience. Television channels, newspapers, magazines, and social media outlets all covered their message of opposition to the injustice Hmong people had faced for decades. At this meeting, "A particularly powerful moment occurred when one of the media representatives asked, 'How many in the room believe that Cha Vang's death was a hate crime?' and nearly every hand went up in the air," reported Wameng Moua in *Hmong Today*.

These cases involving hunters also led the Wisconsin Department of Natural Resources to create a Hmong liaison position to help Hmong hunters understand unfamiliar conventions, such as bag limits, hunting seasons, and property boundaries. The incidents also led to discussion of publication of Wisconsin hunting regulations in other languages, but due to budget constraints, no plans were made at that time to print a Hmong-language version.

The case against Nichols was ongoing when another high-profile incident of racism sparked more outrage from the Hmong. On February 15, 2007, a law professor at the University of Wisconsin–Madison made offensive remarks about Hmong people during a lecture on the legal system and minorities. The seven Hmong students in class wrote a letter to the dean of the law school in which they outlined five complaints against the professor who had made the derogatory comments and asked the university to take action to foster a more welcoming environment. The letter read in part, "We cannot accept the racially hostile environment created by these comments. Therefore, we ask that Professor [Leonard] Kaplan apologize to the class, acknowledging the stereotypes they promote and their inaccuracies. In light of these comments, the events affecting the Hmong community in Wisconsin and the University of Wisconsin's imperative to promote as open a learning environment as possible, we ask that the administration take proactive and concrete steps to prevent the occurrence of intolerant or racist acts and the environment which fosters them."

The email was forwarded widely around campus and obtained by media outlets, heightening racial tensions that were already strained over the hunting incident. Some students and professors defended the professor, saying his remarks were misquoted, taken out of context, or that intellectual freedom should take precedence over students' feelings. Other students saw the professor's comments as ignorant and offensive, perpetuating racial stereotypes. The dean of the law school agreed that the comments were inappropriate and did not conform to the school's expectations. UW Chancellor John Wiley met with the Hmong community in 2007 in an effort to heal the relationship, and the university convened a committee to address Hmong concerns. Afterward, Wiley approved one of their recommendations, to support the creation of a Hmong Studies program at UW–Madison to meet the needs of Hmong American students and to raise cultural awareness of the Hmong.

However, tensions arose again in 2010 when UW–Madison hired a Hmong Studies faculty member who, in the eyes of the Hmong community, was not culturally or linguistically qualified, and Hmong com-

munity leaders felt left out of the hiring process. Their continued advocacy led the university to approve a tenure-track position in 2012, and
this time the recruitment process included the input of Hmong community members and students. In April of 2013, Yang Sao Xiong, who
received his PhD from the University of California–Los Angeles, was
hired for the position. More than 450 people attended a community
reception to celebrate the Hmong community's long journey and to welcome Xiong to Wisconsin.

It took a lot of hard work on the part of many people, both Hmong
and non-Hmong, to see some good come out of the violence and racial
antipathy that dominated Wisconsin headlines for years. The Wisconsin
Department of Natural Resources, leaders from UW–Madison, the Wisconsin United Coalition of Mutual Assistance Association, and members
of the 1.5 generation all worked together to work toward a better understanding. A Hmong sports club opened in Sheboygan as a place where
outdoors enthusiasts of all races could come together and share common
interests. The club holds presentations and events, which are seen as
opportunities for Hmong and white hunters and fisherman to talk about
their differences and enjoy their shared passion for the outdoors. Moreover, the Wisconsin DNR decided to hire Hmong wardens to better
serve Hmong sportsmen and prevent future racial violence in the woods.

The deep rift that racial animosities precipitated between the
Hmong and white communities began to close only when media attention forced Hmong and white leadership to confront racism on open
ground. Today, though some Hmong parents and elders still encourage
young people to stay quiet and patient in the face of racism, 1.5-genera-
tion Hmong are stepping up to the plate and calling for justice. Hmong
of the 1.5 generation speak fluent English, push for civil liberties, and in
some cases have staked their right to a place in the community by running for public office. The Hmong studies program at the University of
Wisconsin–Madison is a success story made possible by the hard work
and community advocacy of 1.5-generation Hmong.

❧❧

## CIVIC PARTICIPATION

Hmong refugees arrived in Wisconsin with I-94 cards, which are legal refugee status cards authorized by US Citizenship and Immigration Services. After two years, refugees were eligible to apply for a permanent green card. After five years, any refugee without a criminal record could apply for citizenship. The long and costly path to citizenship is a difficult one for many Hmong to follow. Aspiring citizens must speak and write English well and have extensive knowledge of US history and culture. The cost and language barriers kept some Hmong from attempting it, while others held out hope that they eventually would be able to return to Laos. The 2010 Census showed that only 57 percent of Hmong in Wisconsin were naturalized as citizens. Proud of their status, these Hmong citizens recognize the responsibilities that come with it. Hmong are often eager to exercise their right to vote. Studying for and passing the required oral exams was very difficult for most of them, so they use their privileges whenever possible. The first wave of Hmong who arrived in 1975 cast their first vote, for either Walter Mondale or Ronald Reagan, in the 1980 presidential election. A decade later, 1.5-generation Hmong were motivated by a sense of civic duty to become involved in local and regional politics. From 1992 to 2008, seven Hmong men ran for public office in Wisconsin. They ran for school board, alder, mayor, circuit judge, city council, and seats in the state assembly.

Thai Vue, who fled Laos with his wife and infant in 1978 and went on to earn a degree from Western Wisconsin Technical College, was elected to the school board in La Crosse in 1993. It was not the first time that a Hmong man had run for a similar political post, as Charles Vue ran unsuccessfully for school board in Eau Claire in 1992. Thai Vue's victory inspired others to seek public office. In the mid-1990s, attorney Koua Vang unsuccessfully ran twice for circuit court judge in Madison. In 1997, Bon Xiong, while still in his early twenties, was appointed as alderman in Appleton and won. Joe Bee Xiong, a former child soldier in Laos who became a reserve police officer and social worker in Wisconsin, secured a city council seat in Eau Claire in 1996 and ran unsuccessfully for state representative in 2006. Ya Yang was elected to the school board and city council in Wausau in 1992, though he lost his bid for mayor four years later. In 2001, Shwaw Vang was elected to the board of the Madison Metropolitan School District, serving two terms. Finally, in 2008 Peng Her made an unsuccessful bid for state assembly. In 2015, as a business owner with years of involvement on the local Economic Development Committee and Hmong Chamber of Commerce, he ran unsuccessfully for Madison City Council. In a questionnaire for the *Capital Times*, he wrote: "I came to the U.S. in 1976 as a refugee from Laos due to the Hmong's alliance with the U.S. during the Vietnam War. I came here with nothing but the clothes on my back and the drive to succeed. I was taught English by the wife of the school's janitor in the janitor's closet. I put myself through college working for Pella Windows, where I learned the value of hard work next to parents working to support their families."

Whether they won or lost at the ballot box, aspiring Hmong politicians attracted positive local and statewide visibility to Hmong communities just by throwing their hats into the political arena. Hmong often ran for office without political experience, campaign volunteers, financial backing, or name recognition. Candidates spent their own money or relied on financial support from their extended families and friends. In the end, most of the Hmong who ran for office did so because they felt an obligation to improve the quality of life for themselves and their neighbors and to bridge the gap between the Hmong and white communities.

The Hmong also saw politics as a vehicle to drive social and cultural change for the better. Hmong community leaders and Lao Family Community of Milwaukee successfully lobbied their state legislator to introduce a Hmong Cultural Center bill. The bill passed, but Governor Jim Doyle vetoed it in 2003 because of its last-minute addition to the budget. Undeterred, Hmong advocacy groups continued to pressure legislators and the Doyle administration, and a new version of the bill passed later that year, designating $2.5 million in state bonding with additional funding to be raised from donors. A feasibility study followed, but the donor campaign was unsuccessful, and the cultural center was never built.

## EDUCATIONAL ADVOCATES

Many people believe that education is the key to success in America. My parents thought so, and Hmong parents and young people today are keenly aware that education is more important than ever. In Wisconsin and elsewhere, those with a good education have access to promising career opportunities. Over the years, Hmong who have studied hard and graduated from colleges and universities, including myself, have found personal fulfillment and success in the workforce.

While some of the first wave of Hmong refugees spoke some English due to their work with the CIA, many later Hmong refugees could not. Some could not write or read their native language either. The American system of education was as foreign to them as the cheddar cheese they hid away to avoid offending the sponsors who served it. As a result, the first group of Hmong students brokered cultural transactions between school and home. Hmong students in these cases became the teachers and their parents their pupils. It did not take long for Hmong parents to realize the value of education. Yang Dao, the first Hmong to earn a PhD in Laos, often made speeches at community gatherings extolling the virtues and benefits of education. Inspired Hmong parents made big plans for their boys and girls, calling for them to study hard. With love and guidance, Hmong parents pressured their children to do well in the classroom. Parents made sure their children understood that by doing well in school, they were fulfilling the legacies of their parents and grandparents, those who had made great sacrifices in Laos and Thailand to bring their families to America.

The first group of Hmong to attend school in Wisconsin had a very different experience from that of their US counterparts. Most Hmong refugee students could not speak or read a word of English, although many learned French and Laotian in Laos and Thai when living in refugee camps. English was to them a second, third, or even fourth language. By the time some students managed to overcome language barriers, they had grown too old to be permitted to attend public schools. Other Hmong students had to leave school to find work and support their families financially.

Later Hmong students, especially at schools with only a handful in attendance, were enrolled in an ESL class. While these classes were supposed to help English-language learners succeed, a secondary purpose seemed to be to eliminate the distraction of serving Hmong students in a regular classroom. The resulting isolation caused many Hmong students to be emotionally stressed. "It was hard for me," said Kazia, a sixteen-year-old Hmong student in California, quoted in *Career Development with Hmong Women*, a 1995 publication of the Madison Center on Education and Work. "I want to read and write English but the kids at school would make fun of me for taking ESL classes and made me feel ashamed for being Hmong."

At school, Hmong students had to be learners and teachers. Hmong students like me had to work with teachers who did not understand the Hmong and were ill-equipped to help Hmong refugees find their way through the school system. I had to teach teachers about Hmong culture and inform them why the Hmong had come to Wisconsin. On top of that, I had so many questions: Which teacher can help me? Is it okay to ask questions in class? Where do I sit in the classroom? Where do I sit at lunch? I was afraid to ask teachers for help for fear of being rude, as I was taught to obey and listen to people in authority, not to question them.

At first, traditional Hmong attitudes toward gender influenced how young Hmong men and women spent their time at school. Girls and boys were expected to fill disparate, prescribed roles at home and in the community. Many Hmong girls were due home immediately after school to start cooking and cleaning. It was okay if Hmong boys stayed after school for sports or other activities. In the same vein, it was considered orthodox for boys to attend college but out of the ordinary for girls to do the same. Therefore, the first generation of Hmong female students who wished to earn a college degree had to prevail over entrenched gender norms. In choosing education over marriage, these same women had to put up with harsh gossip and chatter from disapproving voices in their social circles. The pressure to conform was enough to dissuade some Hmong women from ever attending college.

During their years in school, Hmong students, grappling with the difficulties of assimilation and acculturation, inevitably began to ask many important questions about themselves and their culture. Hmong students not only had to ask themselves what they wanted to be when they grew up, but they also had to ask: Who am I? Who are the Hmong? Why have the Hmong come to Wisconsin and the United States? How much should we let go of our Hmong culture? How can I fit in at school and still find acceptance at home?

As they searched for answers, many who were too young to remember it were told the history of their refugee journey to Wisconsin. At the same time, inquisitive adolescent Hmong learned about the Secret War in Laos and the five-thousand-year history of their origins near the Yellow River in China. The answers to their questions came with more than some young Hmong bargained for. Secondary trauma, a type of trauma experienced by listeners when harrowing stories are told, had painful effects on the teenage Hmong still unsure of their place in Wisconsin. Some of these young people ignored their pain as best they could, while others expressed what they were feeling through art. One can get a better idea of what these youth went through by reading *Bamboo Among the Oaks*, a 2002 anthology of Hmong stories on the topic of what various writers believe it means to be Hmong in America.

By the mid-1980s, the first wave of Hmong students started showing up in university classrooms across Wisconsin. Their numbers increased slightly by the 1990s. Hmong students at the time were viewed as bookish and not very active politically. That stereotype, like so many others, proved untrue. Hmong college students organized the Hmong American Student Association (HASA) to provide Hmong students with a support system as they navigated the financial, academic, and social challenges of university life. On the campuses of UW–Stout, UW–Oshkosh, UW–Madison, UW–Milwaukee, and UW–Stevens Point, Hmong students established satellite branches of the HASA, which eventually took the shape of a statewide coalition. During conferences held at UW–Stout, UW–Oshkosh, and UW–Madison, the parents of Hmong students, along with Hmong community members, learned more about each university and what it was doing to serve its Hmong population. Bilingual staff, either Hmong or Southeast Asian, were hired to provide support for this group of first-generation college students.

During the early 2000s, HASA members began to attend national Asian and Hmong conferences. In fact, most attendees at the biannual Hmong National Development Conference were HASA students there to represent their student organizations, to network, and to sharpen their leadership skills. Some members of HASA expanded their reach and began to take up issues of international human rights. At the local level,

HASA members in Wisconsin began to effect change by supporting Hmong businesses and joining Hmong community advocacy groups.

Many in the first wave of Hmong students who eventually made it to college focused not only on their own futures but on the futures of the next generation too. Hmong college students provided invaluable guidance as mentors. The first wave of students taught the second how to best go through the school system and how to get the support they needed at home and elsewhere. Many first-wave Hmong college students, myself included, spoke to high school students at graduation parties or other events. Together with HASA staff and Hmong college graduates, college students shared their experiences and wisdom with those who would soon find themselves away from home and in need of good advice. Parents took as much away from these events as teenagers did. Parents were reassured to know that they were sending their children to places with a significant and established Hmong presence.

As a greater number of Hmong students started to attend universities in Wisconsin, universities responded by hiring Hmong faculty and staff. UW–Eau Claire recruited several Hmong to develop and direct a precollege program for minority students. The aim of the program is to get Hmong and other minority high school students more prepared for college so they are less likely to drop out or do poorly during their first few semesters. Furthermore, departments and programs at UW–Eau Claire, UW–Green Bay, UW–La Crosse, UW–Stevens Point, UW–Milwaukee, UW–Whitewater, and UW–Madison hired Hmong faculty. They did not do so without controversy, as staff and faculty at some of these universities pushed back against Hmong appointments. Despite bumps in the road such as the one at UW–Madison, the Hmong in Wisconsin have, by any measure, achieved great things in education over the last forty years. There is more work to be done, however. It is important that the next generation of Hmong children stay motivated to do well in school, as there remain impediments to their success. These include decreased federal financial support for low-income children, as many Hmong students are children of the working poor. The Hmong community is also very young and consequently has a limited—but growing—number of educated young men and women around to mentor and provide support for Hmong children and teens.

Educated first-wave Hmong refugees are today the backbone of the Hmong community in Wisconsin. Our success is in large part attributable to the support and love we had from our parents. We were also very motivated to succeed, not only for ourselves but for others as well. We knew we were responsible for keeping our parents' and grandparents' legacies alive in America, and we took this charge very seriously. I am proud of what we have achieved and of the standard we have set for the next generation of Hmong students to follow. At times, we had to force ourselves to come out of our shells and speak up to get what we needed. While many of us would have preferred to stay silent and focus on our studies, we knew we had to be a voice for the voiceless.

Our success does not guarantee the future, though. I constantly ask myself: Will future generations of Hmong students rise to the challenge and study hard? Will they become mentors? Unless we as a society make our children and their education a priority, I am afraid that some Hmong children will be permanently left behind.

## PRIDE IN FARMING

The Hmong who came to Wisconsin practiced an agrarian lifestyle in Laos. Thus, when the Hmong took up farming in Wisconsin, outdoor manual labor and hard work were nothing new to them. Many Hmong found a source of strength in farming, as it gave them purpose and reminded them of their homes in Laos. Other Hmong, mostly young people, learned quickly that manual labor was not for them.

In the early 1980s, many newly arrived Hmong families, including my own, performed seasonal labor in the spring and summer. We worked on cucumber and strawberry farms in Waupaca, New London, and Stevens Point. In Dane and Jefferson Counties, we detasseled corn. Some Hmong harvested wild ginseng in Wausau. On weekends, teenagers worked in the fields alongside their parents and elders to earn extra money. I was one of many unhappy teens who had to leave the house at four o'clock in the morning to start harvesting cucumbers before sunrise.

It did not take long for the Hmong to find local farmers' markets around the state. Hmong who grew fruit and vegetables in their backyards or on a rented plot began to sell produce at these markets. According to Larry John, a staff member at the Dane County Farmers' Market, the first Hmong vendor joined the DCFM in 1992. By 1993, the number had risen to 33 Hmong vendors. The number has grown steadily since. By 2010, of the 275 Dane County vendors, more than 40 were Hmong. For some Hmong, selling vegetables at the farmers' market is about more than just growing produce and making money. Many Hmong take a satisfaction in farming that fills a void in their lives. WaSeng Ly of Kimberly shared that when he arrived to Wisconsin in 1976, he was homesick and feeling lost. "One day our sponsor took us to his garden and gave us a hoe. We were able to plant the seeds we brought and harvested our own vegetables to eat. The hoe and garden returned to me my self-confidence." Others find therapy in farming as well. When Hmong struggling to learn English felt their confidence and self-worth waning, they regained lost dignity when they had something to show for all their hard work.

Gardening was as much an escape from work as it was difficult labor. Hmong who worked stressful evening blue-collar jobs, such as stacking cardboard boxes on an assembly line, operating machinery, or putting labels on boxes, enjoyed working in their gardens in their free time. The garden was familiar to them, a place where they could relax and reflect on their new life. Working in the garden also strengthened familial bonds that had been tried on the journey to America from Laos and Thailand. To garden effectively and sell produce successfully at the farmers' market required teamwork. Time spent planting, weeding, gathering, and traveling to farmers' markets inevitably brought families closer together. More often than not, children as young as twelve worked as cashiers and interpreters at vegetable stands until their parents, uncles, aunts, or grandparents learned enough English to go without their interpreters. Many of today's Hmong learned English and expanded their vocabularies while working in their produce stands.

Of course, the Hmong had more pressing and practical reasons to garden and sell fruits and vegetables. Hmong families were always in need of money. In the 1990s, it was not uncommon for Hmong parents to work more than one job to support families with five or six children. Some families turned to farming and gardening to supplement their incomes.

What do Hmong farmers sell at their produce stands? The fare was somewhat exotic at first: bitter melons, purple beans, mustard greens, squash leaves, snow pea leaves, chili peppers, and herbs such as cilantro, basil, and mint. Many of these items did not sell well. Wisconsinites for the most part did not know how to eat or cook with the produce the Hmong offered. Making matters worse, Hmong vendors did not speak English well enough to tell their customers how to enjoy and prepare Hmong cuisine. To counter these difficulties, the Hmong made changes in their produce plots and at their produce stands. Green onions, green beans, potatoes, spinach, strawberries, and raspberries soon lined Hmong booths at farmers' markets. The Hmong lost something in their gains, though, when they started to offer the same merchandise as their neighbors, as the switch frustrated those looking to buy traditional Hmong herbs and vegetables.

Today, Hmong produce vendors operate at farmers' markets throughout the state. In big markets and small, from Madison to Kaukauna, it is likely that wherever there is a farmers' market, there are Hmong selling their goods. Since the 1990s, when Hmong gardeners started selling produce in Dane County, the Hmong have branched out to places such as Summit, Sheboygan, and Manitowoc. Hmong farmers work hard to grow their produce and sometimes travel far to bring it to market. A good number of Hmong farmers who sell at the farmers' market on the Capitol Square in Madison travel from as far away as Eau Claire. Although the drive is long, it is worth it to take advantage of the customer base in Madison, as the farmers' market on the Capitol Square is one of the largest in the country.

It is important to mention that the Hmong have had agricultural success away from the farmers' markets as well. In the late 1980s and the early 1990s, Hmong families in Wisconsin began to grow ginseng. The ginseng business was lucrative enough to draw aspiring Hmong ginseng growers from Minnesota and Michigan to Wisconsin. The perennial herb has many uses: it is found in beauty products, beverages, supplements, and food. Yee Vang was one of the first Hmong to cultivate ginseng in Wisconsin, doing so in Wausau. Ginseng farmers such as Vang now grow ginseng on farms up to fifty acres in size, selling their harvest to Chinese wholesalers who buy and pick up the ginseng on site. The ginseng industry received a boost in 2017 when ginseng was named as the state herb of Wisconsin.

The first wave of Hmong refugees in Wisconsin took up gardening and farming as a way to cope with what they had lost and to get their bearings on the future. Their teenage children, however, quickly learned that farming was not their cup of tea. Where their parents took strength and comfort from the soil, teenagers found in the land good reasons to study hard and one day get a white-collar job. Kaying Xiong, the first Hmong principal of Randall Elementary School in Eau Claire, decided early on that farming was not for her. Speaking as one of four keynote panelists at the Hmong National Conference in Milwaukee in 2004, Xiong recalled that her time spent picking cucumbers with her parents imbued in her a desire for more. As Xiong put it, "I could not see myself pick[ing] cucumber[s] for the rest of my life." Many first-wave Hmong professionals have similar stories to share. Given that fewer numbers of young Hmong are gardening and farming, it is likely that the Hmong presence at farmers' markets will decline in the years to come. Some Hmong parents hope that Hmong farmers will soon bring back authentic Hmong ingredients to their stands, but as it stands, the number of Hmong farmers will probably continue to shrink because many of the younger-generation Hmong lack the skills, endurance, and to a greater extent, interest.

## ECONOMIC ENTERPRISE OF THE 1.5 GENERATION

The Hmong arrived in Wisconsin with little money and no knowledge of the US economy. Although they received some financial help from churches and sponsors, Hmong refugees were very poor. Many Hmong did not see their situation as permanent, though. Hmong parents and elders tended to look beyond their privation, choosing instead to focus on a future in which their children and grandchildren would join the ranks of a different class. Their vision proved prophetic in some cases, as ambitious Hmong children and teenagers, including myself, found their way out of poverty.

Money was a relatively new concept to the first Hmong in Wisconsin, since they had little use for a monetary system in Laos, where they had lived in peace apart from other ethnic groups. The Hmong agrarian lifestyle revolved around manual labor and economic self-sufficiency. Within close-knit clan structures, the Hmong practiced cooperative farming and bartered goods with one another, with every able person contributing something. Healthy persons who could not provide ade-quate food, clothing, and shelter for themselves and their families were considered lazy. If a family fell under public scrutiny, their harvest might be evaluated for its quality and quantity. Those not pulling their weight were also in danger of being ostracized by the community. Families who were in their fields before sunrise and still in them at sunset often tried to marry their children to families that did the same.

When the French came to Laos in 1893, they brought with them a new economy of exchange. The Hmong traded with the French colonists, exchanging rice or opium for household goods such as salt, cloth, and silver. During the Vietnam War, small storefronts popped up in Hmong villages, where the Hmong sold basic household items such as soap, shoes, cloth, and silverware. In Long Chieng, where the CIA oper-ated an air base and headquarters during the Secret War, the Hmong sold food and goods out of booths and stores at the morning market or in front of homes. At Long Chieng and in small villages, the Hmong learned to use the Laotian kip, the national currency of Laos. When the Hmong were forced from their villages to refugee camps in Thailand, a few enterprising Hmong saw an opportunity to make money. With finan-cial support from American, French, and Australian backers, Hmong vendors purchased household items and produce from outside the camps, then sold their products to refugees.

The first Hmong in Wisconsin brought with them a mindset of eco-nomic self-sufficiency. It was what they had known in Laos. Many dreamed from the start of owning a home and business. Some would eventually do so, but not before they had to swallow their pride and accept help from others. Hmong leaned on Aid to Families with Dependent Children, a federal assistance program that provided fund-ing for basic needs to families, including much-needed food stamps to Hmong parents who were working part time-while attending school to improve their English.

Nearly all the 1.5-generation Hmong grew up in low-income hous-ing. A number of them were the de facto heads of their households because they had a better command of English than their parents and elders. Hmong children and teenagers were often forced to grow up quickly and assume adult responsibilities before they reached adulthood. Mee Moua, a former Minnesota state senator who was raised in Apple-ton, described her responsibilities at home in Peter and Connie Roop's book *The Hmong in America*: "Being the oldest in my family with the knowledge of English, I act in many respects on behalf of my parents, my relatives, and above all my community. I accompany my siblings to medical clinics, help my parents look for an apartment and jobs, fill out forms and documents for my clan members, and at times serve as an interpreter for my community." The manner in which Hmong children parented their parents during the early years of Hmong resettlement is indicative of the role reversals and stark cultural changes that accompanied the Hmong move to America.

For their part, the older generation demonstrated the values of hard work and resiliency and, through their effort, helped ensure their children would have better educational and work opportunities than they had. In their blue-collar jobs at factories, Hmong men and women worked hard and often outperformed their coworkers. Many held two or even three jobs at once to provide for their families and their future. Where the median Hmong household income was $13,974 in 1989, that number rose to $35,898 in 1999, then to $49,000 in 2010, according to US Census data.

By the early 1990s, members of the 1.5 generation of Hmong who arrived as teenagers to Wisconsin in the early 1980s had stepped into the economy as employees, business owners, and homeowners. Some worked for corporations, while others took over a family business from their parents or set out on a venture of their own. A few earned advanced degrees and started their careers as medical doctors, dentists, or attorneys.

Whereas the first Hmong businesses, such as Asian wholesale grocery stores and ethnic restaurants, were created to serve the needs of the Hmong community, businesses aimed at the larger community, such as insurance agencies, beauty salons, and auto body repair shops, followed. Educated and ambitious 1.5-generation Hmong expanded the number of Hmong businesses in different ways. For instance, my husband and I opened the restaurant Taste of Asia in Madison, offering a diverse menu of Lao, Chinese, Vietnamese, and Thai foods. For five years, he ran the restaurant during the day and cared for our children in the evening while I worked full-time at the State Refugee Office during the day and worked evenings and weekends at the restaurant. In Green Bay, the Kong family opened the first Hmong-owned auto dealership in Wisconsin. The Egg Roll Plus restaurant began to serve Hmong egg rolls to the people of Eau

Claire. On East Washington Street in Madison, Hmong Restaurant became the first restaurant in the city to serve a fully Hmong menu. Hmong of the 1.5 generation established similar restaurants in Sheboygan and La Crosse. Rhino Foods in Milwaukee offered customers the chance to take Hmong cooking home with them, selling ready-to-eat traditional Hmong cuisine such as *ncuav pob kwv* (corn cake), *ncuav nplej thiab ncauv pia* (rice and wheat cake), *hnyuv ntxwm mov* (rice sausage), and *taum paj* (fresh tofu). Phongsavan Asian Market opened in Milwaukee with a food court, a grocery store, and other clothing and video shops. In Sturgeon Bay, Po Lo entered the beverage market when he and his family opened Lo Artisan Distillery, crafters of traditional Hmong rice spirits now sold in liquor stores across Wisconsin, Minnesota, and California. Elsewhere, Hmong women also became entrepreneurs, running beauty shops and small restaurants. Perhaps the most creative business idea came out of Wausau, where the Lee family started a shoe company to create jobs for Hmong women with a talent for sewing.

By the turn of the millennium, the Hmong were attaining higher levels of education and gained access to other corners of the American economy. Many found work in the health, legal, and financial professions. Some work as aides, interpreters, and nurses, doing what they can not only to make a living but also to accommodate the needs of other Hmong. Dr. David Blong Lee, a graduate of Marquette University, who resettled in Sheboygan in the late 1990s from Wat Thamkrabok, opened the first Hmong dental office in Sheboygan. Dr. Alex Thor opened a dental clinic of his own in Sun Prairie, and Dr. Cha Lee started a health care clinic in Milwaukee. Dr. Salad Vang did the same in Appleton in 2010. Zoua Yang owns nursing homes in the Fox Cities area and has helped others to open similar businesses elsewhere. In Madison, Shoua Yang and her husband, Song Lue Vue, started SoSiab Homecare to serve Southeast Asian and refugee elders. Eternity Homecare, owned by Vang Thao, operates statewide and provides home healthcare to older Southeast Asians in Wisconsin. Highlander Home Health, a Hmong business out of Milwaukee, does the same kind of work and employs more than a dozen people. Tou Lor of Madison opened Midway Transit, a transportation company. The dozen Hmong who went to law school practice at firms throughout the state. Some opened their own offices in Madison, Green Bay, and Appleton. Heather Ly, a CPA, was the first to start a Hmong accounting firm, Ly Certified Public Accounting, in Milwaukee.

The economic contributions of the Hmong will likely continue to increase as 1.5-generation Hmong make strides in their respective careers and industries. Nevertheless, it would be a terrible mistake to assume that because the Hmong have made economic strides over the last several decades, theirs is a community no longer in need of help. Many uneducated Hmong still live in poverty and require the same kinds of care and public assistance that helped high-achieving Hmong of the 1.5 generation get on their feet.

When the Hmong succeed economically, it is good for everyone in Wisconsin. Thriving Hmong businesses boost the economy and create jobs for Hmong and non-Hmong alike. As consumers, homeowners, business owners, and tenants, the Hmong have a significant economic foothold in Wisconsin. In 2000, the buying power of Hmong in Wisconsin was $234 million, according to the US Census. In the same year, Hmong paid $3.3 million in real estate taxes and $1.3 million in rental payments, and Hmong home ownership hit 48.2 percent, up from 9.9 percent in 1990. Hmong homeownership has continued to rise, reaching 55 percent in 2010. These examples of success have defied the US government's original supposition that the Hmong people were too primitive to succeed in the American economy. That they had the chance to prove themselves is in large part due to the lobbying efforts of the refugee advocates who worked to allow their resettlement. Today, the 1.5-generation Hmong are paying it forward, as their taxes go toward helping new refugees come to the United States.

## TRADITIONAL RELIGIOUS BELIEFS
## VS. CHRISTIANITY

The Hmong New Year celebrates the end of the harvest season and in Laos takes place during the full moon at the end of the twelfth month of the lunar calendar. In Wisconsin, it is celebrated on various dates in different communities due to seasonal weather, availability of space, and employment schedules. On the eve of the Hmong New Year, Hmong who practice traditional beliefs are busy with rituals. On this night, a shaman or elder performs the *hu plig* to call home wayward souls. A bowl of uncooked rice and burning incense is placed on a small table by the front door in front of the soul caller. Next to the rice bowl is a bigger bowl filled with uncooked eggs and a live chicken in a cardboard box, which is later butchered and cooked. When the second stage of the *hu plig* is complete, the soul caller examines the chicken's feet, head, and tongue to ensure all souls are home. The eggs are then given to every family member. Prior to the soul calling ritual, community members rotate through the ritual of *lwm qaib*, in which they leave behind bad deeds and spirits from the past year and welcome in a fresh start. Afterward and prior to dinner, the husband or other elder performs the *ntov pob ntoo* or *laig dab* to call upon three generations of ancestors to eat with and protect the family.

The tradition of soul calling is one of the many cultural practices that the Hmong brought with them to the United States from Laos. To a large extent, the Hmong in Wisconsin still worship in the traditional ways by practicing animism, the belief that natural objects such as trees, rivers, mountains, and rocks contain spirits and that human souls remain in harmony with them. In addition to soul calling, traditional Hmong wedding and funeral rites are still performed by a significant number of Hmong in Wisconsin.

Christianity came to Laos well before Americans did. Jesuit missionaries arrived in 1642. More than two centuries later, in 1880, Presbyterians began to preach their faith to the Hmong. The Swiss Brethren arrived in 1902, followed by missionaries from the Christian and Missionary Alliance, a Protestant denomination, in 1929. Early efforts were largely unsuccessful, as the Hmong saw them as a threat to their own culture and traditions, but the missionaries made progress in the 1950s when they targeted Hmong community members who needed assistance, whether from illness, poverty, or lack of a support system. These converts then would help to convert other Hmong, sometimes entire families or villages. In one six-month period, seventeen hundred Hmong converted to Christianity in what became known as the "people's movement." Conversion rates spiked again during the Secret War in the mid-1960s in northern Laos, where an American Bible school was established to train pastors and evangelists, according to Timothy T. Vang, author of *Coming Full Circle*.

The Hmong continued to accept Christianity during the Vietnam War as well as in the Thai refugee camps and in the United States. In Wisconsin, the Hmong joined Lutheran, Catholic, Christian and Missionary Alliance, Presbyterian, and other Christian denominations for a variety of reasons. Some did so out of respect for their church sponsors, or because they sought assistance or acceptance from these groups, rather than from a genuine alteration in their beliefs. Occasionally, Hmong suffering from an illness that could not be cured by traditional means converted as a last resort. Another compelling reason, suggested by Dia Cha, a professor at St. Cloud State University in Minnesota, is that descendants of Hmong men killed during the Secret War did not have knowledge of Hmong rituals and traditions. With the thousands of Hmong men killed during the Secret War died a wealth of religious knowledge that never made it to America. Some Hmong Christians continued to practice diluted versions of their own traditions as well. Some Catholic Hmong, for example, still believe in soul calling, and others continue to celebrate some form of Hmong New Year through their adopted church.

Some Hmong converts ended up returning to their own traditions once they became more settled in their new homes and less dependent on their Christian sponsors, and the number of Hmong Christians in Wisconsin declined or plateaued through the 1990s. But several denominations continued to attract new Hmong membership by fundraising and building new churches in states with large Hmong populations such as Wisconsin. Concern grew among some Hmong that their children had increasingly limited opportunities to absorb traditional religious knowledge or appreciate the traditional practices of their own culture, leading to a renewed and invigorated interest in preserving animism. A few Hmong MAAs, Hmong scholars, and others now teach young people the value of their own traditions and the intricacies of their rituals. As Hmong communities have become more well established, it also has become easier for them to continue the tradition of the elaborate and expensive Hmong funerals. The sound of the *qeej* instrument can even be heard at some Hmong funerals, as groups of young boys throughout Wisconsin are learning to play the instrument at Kajsiab House in Madison and elsewhere.

Weddings are another area where Hmong traditions have largely given way to more modern, Americanized conventions. For example, traditional Hmong ceremonies featured a musical chanting ritual called *hais zaj tshoob* during which significant aspects of the wedding were communicated, such as asking for permission to enter the bride's house, asking for the bride's marriage negotiators, or accepting the marriage agreement. This traditional chanting ritual has become rare, cutting the wedding time in half, although the wedding still lasts an entire weekend and follows a traditional pattern. Typically, the groom arrives at the bride's house on Friday evening to ask for the parents' permission or negotiate the marriage agreement. On Saturday, family and guests celebrate with *noj tshoob* (a feast) and formally recognize the couple. On Sunday, the groom's parents hold *tiam mej koob* (a second appreciation feast) to thank the wedding party and formally introduce and welcome the bride to her new family and clan.

Change is inevitable, though. The rituals performed today are not the same as those performed in Wisconsin forty years ago. Nor do they mirror exactly the traditions carried out in Laos for centuries before the Hmong diaspora. Celebrations of the Hmong New Year, Hmong funerary practices, and soul calling rituals are all, at least in some ways, different. Young families, for example, out of convenience or because they lack space, rarely perform soul calling rituals. They might place only a few eggs in the bowl during the *hu plig* ritual instead of one egg per family member needed for a *hu plig*. Others forgo the *hu plig* altogether. Increasingly, young Hmong couples who are less familiar with traditional rituals of their culture choose to forgo them entirely.

## LOOKING FORWARD

The course of Hmong history forever changed as a result of the United States' covert operation in Laos. The Hmong who supported the United States were marked for extinction by the Communists. Whereas some Hmong parents were hesitant to resettle in countries such as America, their children embraced the opportunity to start a new life as refugees.

In Wisconsin and elsewhere, Hmong refugees and their children began their lives all over again—learning a new language and culture while embracing new neighbors and working hard to be independent. Despite feeling as though they were going against the fast current of a river, many parents invested all their hopes and energies in their children. Although Hmong parents were illiterate in English, they knew that education was the key to success in their new home—Wisconsin and America. Therefore, they encouraged and did what they could to support their children to obtain an education. With hard work and a desire to succeed, Hmong children have achieved success in educational, economic, and business development.

Today, the 1.5 generation of Hmong thrive as taxpayers—they became self-sufficient, bought houses, and created businesses. Most important, the children learned and became the buffer that spoke out and protected their parents and community against racial injustice. Despite cultural, racial, and ethnic discrimination, the Hmong remain a vibrant community using their extended families and clan systems. They continue to bring positive changes to both their ethnic and mainstream communities as Wisconsinites—they stimulate the economy wherever they live, are role models for others, and continue to improve their civic participation.

In the past four decades, while the 1.5 generation's Hmong American children are moving on with their new lives as Wisconsinites, many elders and parents still dream that one day they will be able to return to Laos, their homeland. However, since the death of General Vang Pao, this dream is fading away, along with other dreams that someday the Hmong can live in an environment where they can grow their own food, discipline their own children, and govern their own communities. The 1.5 generation of Hmong children grew up to become community and grassroots organizers, faculty members at various Wisconsin universities, nurses and doctors in hospitals and health clinics, and teachers. Other professionals work in city, county, and state government settings, and many Hmong are business owners in various professions. A small number of children born to the 1.5 generation graduated from Ivy League schools. Most important, they began to create a community wherever they lived and became productive citizens.

The future generations of Hmong Americans will continue to thrive and strengthen the fabric of Wisconsin and America should they follow in the footsteps of their parents and grandparents: work hard, have pride in themselves, and build a community wherever they live in America. As a young community, their success will depend heavily on the level of support, guidance, and resources available for Hmong American children.

Victor Xiong

Victor Xiong of Milwaukee raised a family and advocated for the Hmong community while finishing his associate's degree in 1999. Xiong was one of the few Hmong men to receive an education in Laos prior to resettling in Wisconsin.

Kaying Xiong became the first elementary school principal of Hmong descent at Randall Elementary in Eau Claire in 2000. Later, Kaying went on to become the student services director of the Eau Claire Area School District.

A proud Hmong vet-
eran who fought with
the Americans in the Se-
cret War in Laos, Nhia
Thong "Charles" Lor
first resettled in Col-
orado before moving
with his family to Mil-
waukee in 1984. In
2002, the Lor family be-
came the proud owners
of the Hmong Oriental
Market in Madison.

Charles Lor

Charles Vue

Students and staff who participated in the University of Wisconsin–Eau Claire Hmong
Youth Leadership Pre-College Camp from July 21 to August 4, 2002.

Peng Her

Peng Her, a Madison resident who ran for city council and state representative, speaks at a Howard Dean for America rally in 2003 in Washington, DC.

Ge Vue of Kaukauna, Wisconsin, returns to his seat after receiving his degree as part of the Hmong Class of 2004 at Carleton College in Minnesota. The Hmong graduates proudly displayed their Hmong heritage that day by wearing their traditional costumes.

La Crosse Mayor John Medinger with a Hmong community member at the annual Hmong New Year Festival in La Crosse in October 2004. Elected officials are often invited to join Hmong community events.

Staff members of the Sheboygan Hmong Mutual Assistance Association (MAA) in 2004. MAAs are refugee-run nonprofit agencies established as a result of the Refugee Act of 1980. In Wisconsin, most MAAs have been run by Hmong refugees.

Wangchue Dang Moua

Iraq War veteran Neo Lor (middle) on February 2, 2005.

Houa Moua

Nplias Yaj, a farmer, sells vegetables at the Eau Claire Downtown Farmers Market in 2010.

Houa Moua

Nplias Xyooj and Tsav Yeej Lis, pictured in their flower fields in Eau Claire in 2010, are among the Hmong farmers who drive to Madison to sell their produce at the Dane County Farmers' Market on the Capitol Square.

At the Hmong New Year celebration in Madison in 2010, parents from the Hmong Victory Alliance participate in a fashion show to share traditional Hmong costumes with the younger generation. The event is a time to see many traditional Hmong costumes as well as the latest fashions.

Po Lo (left), owner of the Lo Artisan Distillery in Door County, the first Hmong-owned distillery in Wisconsin, is pictured with Mai Zong Vue, Charles Vang, a board member of the Hmong Chamber of Commerce, and Lo's father, Chong Lo, at the Hmong Chamber of Commerce's annual banquet in Milwaukee in 2014.

Hmong community leaders met with the Wisconsin Department of Health Services about Hmong mental health needs on August 6, 2013. From left: Neng Vue, president of the Hmong American Community Association, Menomonie; Kieng Yang, a volunteer with Wisconsin United Coalition of Mutual Assistance Association, Onalakska; Nao Tou Lor, president of Wisconsin Lao Veterans of America, Wisconsin Rapids; Lo Lee, executive director of the Hmong American Partnership of Fox Valley, Appleton; Nhia Long Yang, executive director of the Hmong Community Center, Manitowoc; Koua Vang, executive director of the United Asian Services of Wisconsin, Madison; and Thai Vue, executive director of the Wisconsin United Coalition of Mutual Assistance Association, Onalaska.

Charles Vue

Thirty-six Hmong students attended the two-week Youth Leadership Camp at the University of Wisconsin–Eau Claire in 2019, where they learned about post-secondary options and career paths, participated in Hmong cultural activities, and worked on leadership skills.

# Four Families' Resettlement Stories

❦

## YEE THAO

*Yee Thao is a Madison-area farmer and health professional. She was interviewed by the author.*

Many Hmong farmers are of the older generation who either grew up in Laos or farmed with their parents. That is not the case for Yee Thao. Thao is not your typical Hmong farmer, who tends to be older and shy and to speak broken English or no English. Born in 1980 in Ban Vinai, a refugee camp in Thailand, Yee grew up watching her parents farm. Today, Thao is a thriving farmer in Madison, selling vegetables to more than eighty businesses—mostly high-end restaurants and hotels in Madison. In addition, being younger and speaking English fluently, Thao has become an educator and advocate for Hmong farmers in Wisconsin.

When explaining how she came to be a farmer, Thao recalled that ever since childhood, she has enjoyed playing with dirt and came to love working in bare feet in her garden. She still finds peace and joy by kneeling down, letting her bare feet touch the dirt, and using her hands to mold the dirt like dough. Thao is so convinced that she was born to be a farmer that she joked that her mom must have "conceived her on the farm."

Thao, her parents, three brothers, and four sisters arrived in Wisconsin in 1995, much later than other Hmong refugees, as part of the third wave of Hmong refugee resettlement. Thao arrived as a teenager and started high school at age fifteen with no knowledge of English. Without adequate support at school or at home, she skipped school frequently. For many Hmong girls at the time, a common solution to academic struggles was marriage. Hmong girls were pressured to marry young, as girls older than fifteen would be perceived as old. Through marriage, Hmong girls could demonstrate that they were responsible, reliable, and mature. Therefore, after one year in Madison, Thao was married in 1996 at the age of sixteen. While still a student, she became a wife and a mother and learned to multitask to fulfill all her roles.

As a hard-working individual, Thao found her married life boring and wanted to do something that she enjoyed. She enrolled in and completed a one-year farming program in 1998. Like many in the younger generation, Thao became the interpreter for Hmong parents at a community garden. Her gardening skill and knowledge led her to become the treasurer for the Quann Community Garden. Soon thereafter, she was hired to staff the Community Action Coalition for Southeast Wisconsin, which became the anchor for Hmong farmers to learn and improve their farming services. This position opened Thao's eyes to the needs of the Hmong farmers.

With her passion to help Hmong farmers to succeed, Thao devoted her time to recruiting and helping more Hmong learn about farming in their new home in Wisconsin. While at the Community Action Coalition, Thao met Janet Parker. They brainstormed together regarding the best way to serve Hmong farmers' needs. In 2010, they became involved in a nonprofit, the Farley Center, to support and increase the number of minority farmers. The Farley Center competes for federal grants and trains minorities who are interested in farming.

While many Hmong have a background in farming, they do not necessarily understand all aspects of the farming business—marketing, pricing, and wholesaling. Frustrated to see the lack of such skills causing Hmong farmers to struggle, several staff members from the Farley Center started the Spring Rose Growers Cooperative, a private company, to sell produce at wholesale prices. Thao joined in 2012. Despite the efforts of Thao and others to support Hmong farmers, not many have joined the cooperative because of language and other business barriers, but the wholesale business produced more than $450,000 in three years.

Farming has made up only half of Thao's career, though. During the winter, she works full time as a certified nursing assistant at St. Mary's Hospital in Madison. "I love helping people and being a nursing assistant because, unlike other farmers, I get to scrub my hands so much that my hands are white, so no one believes that I am a farmer," Thao joked. She also attends several farming conferences in the winter, where she is often the only Hmong in attendance. She starts seeding in February, planting in May, and harvesting and selling from July to October—a routine that Thao loves. She works part-time at St. Mary's in addition to working long days on her farm. "I am at my garden all the time—as much as I can afford," she said. Thao joked that now that her two daughters and son are older, she has more time to do what she loves—get down on her bare feet and get dirty.

When asked what motivates her to get up early and do what she does, Thao explained that there is so much she can teach older Hmong farmers about succeeding in the field here in Wisconsin. She also hopes to see more diversity in the produce at local farmers' markets by increasing the number of nonwhite vendors. Thao shared with pride that a large group of Asian, Latino, and other ethnic shoppers have frequented the Hilldale Farmers' Market because she and other Hmong farmers sell produce that they enjoy. "Bitter melon, squash leaf, snow pea leaf, and Thai eggplant are big hits for nonwhite customers," Thao explained.

When she first arrived, Thao said she did not expect that a refugee like herself would be able to live a life of peace and prosperity. But despite the educational challenges Thao experienced, she is proud of her achievements. Looking into a promising future, Thao said she would like to return to school to finish her nursing degree and work toward obtaining her organic certification. In addition, Thao would like to continue to help others to become successful farmers. "Teaching the elders to preserve the land is very important to me," Thao explained.

꧁❧❧꧂

# NHIA THONG "CHARLES" LOR

*Nhia Thong "Charles" Lor is a veteran of the Secret War. His family owns a grocery store in Madison. He was interviewed by the author.*

Arriving at Nhia Thong "Charles" Lor's grocery store, the first thing I saw behind his cashier counter was the classic picture—a young soldier carrying a gun as tall as himself, standing in front of a truck. I had seen this boy with a gun many times but did not know who it was. Holding the picture of himself in his hand, Lor talked about his experiences as a young soldier in the Secret Army, his journey as a refugee, and his new life in America.

As is customary, I first went to greet Pao Youa Vang, his wife, in the deli at the back of the store. She handles the deli while Lor manages the rest of the store. Then I returned to begin my interview. Lor and his wife have six children plus a few grandchildren. Known as Charles to his non-Hmong veteran friends, he is called Nhia Thong in the Hmong community. I wanted to ask why he would take an American name but did not want to interrupt his deep thoughts as he talked about his father and uncle.

After his father and uncle died in combat, Lor and his older brother were recruited to join the Secret War in 1969, when Lor was twelve. With a smile on his face, he shared that because of his age and physical size, he could not carry the M-16 rifle, so he did not fight on the front line until he was thirteen and a half. Instead, he stayed in the barracks and prepared food packages, water supplies, and medicine to be sent to soldiers on the front lines.

In 1975, after the Americans airlifted General Vang Pao and his officers, Lor threw away his uniform to avoid being captured and returned to farming and got married. Due to his small size—standing about five feet tall—no one suspected Lor's affiliation with the Secret Army. However, in 1979, Lor, his wife, and other family members fled Laos when they heard about the effort to eliminate any Hmong who supported the United States. The journey to Thailand was difficult because their village was very far from the Mekong River. They and other refugees hid in the jungle and, when they ran out of rice, ate whatever edible food they could find. They moved from one place to another—sometimes every day, sometimes every month. According to Lor, the hardest thing to do was to watch people die of starvation and illness.

In March 1979, they finally reached the bank of the Mekong River and hid until nine o'clock at night to avoid detection by the communist soldiers patrolling the area. To avoid attracting attention, they swam in small groups of five or six people at a time. Lor's wife and mother-in-law did not know how to swim, so they used bamboo poles to float. He tied his two cousins and himself together and then tied his wife and mother-in-law to the group. Together, Lor and his cousins swam and pulled the others. At three o'clock in the morning, after six hours of pulling his family, they reached the Thai shore. At this point, Lor paused in his story to recognize how lucky his group had been. Many other Hmong families who had tried to make the journey had been killed or drowned during the crossing of the river to Thailand.

While telling me this story, Lor took a break to help a customer carry a bag of rice out to the car. When Lor returned, he shared with some pride that he had the assistance of Jerry Daniels, who served as a liaison between the Hmong soldiers and the CIA during the war and afterward worked in the Hmong refugee camps to facilitate their resettlement. Daniels left a written note advocating for Lor with the staff in the Americans' office. Because of the note, when Lor arrived for his resettlement interview, he did not have to answer all the questions to pass the screening test. The staff talked, laughed among themselves, and stamped his application. Unlike thousands of other refugees, Lor had a short stay in the refugee camp.

After arriving in the United States, language was a huge barrier for the Lor family. Lor's cousin, who served as his sponsor, helped them get an apartment in Colorado, where they looked for jobs and applied for public assistance. Lor worked as a janitor at a hotel for two years for $3.25 per hour. In one incident he remembers well, his supervisor became very mad at him because Lor did not know the English terms for *dust pan* and *broom*, so he could not get the items for his supervisor when asked. "I was very sad that day! When I finished all my work, I sat at the hotel stairs and just burst out in tears. I cried and cried—thinking, how was I going to survive in this country like this?"

As newcomers, he and his wife did not know how to drive, so they walked and relied on public transportation—riding a city bus to work, which was a challenge. "There were times when we missed work for a whole day because we got lost," Lor recalled with a smile. "After we found our way back home, the day was over and we were exhausted and frustrated." They walked very far to buy groceries. At the grocery store, they did not know how to communicate with the cashier, so they gave their food stamp booklet to the cashier. The cashier took what was needed and handed the booklet back to them.

With determination, Lor finished a machine-shop class and went to work at a machine shop. As he and his wife struggled, they heard from relatives that Wisconsin offered a better education system than Colorado. Like other Hmong refugees, they relocated to Milwaukee in April 1984. At this point, Lor also made the decision that many refugees and immigrants make to adopt an American name as a way to try to avoid employment discrimination. Lor and his wife also gave American names to their children.

In Milwaukee, Lor and his wife returned to school to learn more English while they worked, volunteered to serve the Hmong communities, and tested out business opportunities. To improve their children's education, in 1990, they moved to Hartford and sent their children to private schools. They worked different shifts so they could transport their children to school daily.

Working hard, they were able to save enough money to pay for their children's education and for a future business start-up. First, they tried renting out properties but lacked maintenance skills. They opened a small auto repair shop for a few years but gave up because they did not know how to fix cars and had to rely on their employees. In 2002, the most viable option was to do what Lor knew how to do best—serve the needs of the community with his management and people skills. They moved to Madison and bought an ethnic community grocery store, renaming it Madison Oriental Market. Lor quit his job and became his own boss. Shortly after he took over the business, his wife quit her job and joined him. While it was a drastic move, Lor felt confident it would make the best use of his skills and allow him to focus on his family, with more time to spend with their six children. On weekends, the children helped out at the store. Lor also hoped the family-owned business would provide a solid foundation for their future.

Lor's children grew up to be educated professionals and business owners themselves. His oldest son went on to own a dental lab in Minnesota, the middle son bought an auto repair shop in Madison, and the youngest son became assistant vice president of the lending department with Chase Bank in Florida. Their oldest daughter became director of Madison School and Community Recreation, where their youngest daughter is also an assistant director, and their middle daughter works as a nurse. Meanwhile, Lor and his wife have found their version of the American dream—working hard every day with no vacation but a life they enjoy.

## XONG SAYAOVONG VANG YANG

*Xong Sayaovong Vang Yang is the owner of Titan Public Safety Solutions in Madison. She was interviewed by the author.*

Xong Sayaovong Vang Yang's middle name is the name of her family's great-great-grandfather, SaYao Vang. It is uncommon for Hmong to add the name of their grandfather or great-grandfather to their last name or middle name, but the practice is gradually gaining traction in America. "Everyone in my family has this middle name so that our lineage can be traced," Yang said.

In April 1976, when she was six years old, Yang's family arrived in Milwaukee, Wisconsin. Her father, Nao Ly S. Vang, was twenty-five years old; her mother, Sao Yang, was twenty-three years old; and her two brothers, Kou and Kao, were four and three. Four more siblings were also born in Milwaukee. Years later, Yang learned from her mother about her family's years as refugees.

Seven Milwaukee-area churches sponsored her family. Some of the church members welcomed them to Milwaukee by waiting for them as they arrived at the airport, holding pictures of the family so they could find one another. Their sponsors brought them to a small home next to the Lutheran Church on Sixth Street and Wisconsin Avenue, where they lived until another home was found. The sponsors came to teach them English, and every week they took her mom to the grocery store. Church members also found her father a job, taught him how to drive, and later gave him a car so he could go to work. Yang's family was fortunate to arrive in the first wave of Hmong refugees, when sponsors were most eager to help them transition to their new environment and life.

Yang said she was too young to remember anything about their early days in Milwaukee, but her mother remembers seeing snow on the ground when they arrived and noticing the large coats people wore when outside. She thought these people were really crazy because it looked so cold. Not knowing the word for snow yet, she called it frost.

Yang's parents do not remember being afraid; they felt safe and taken care of in their new home. Their sponsors provided beds for them to sleep on, clothes for them to wear, and a safe place for them to live. The churches also stocked the pantry with food for the family, but the family did not eat much of it at first, not realizing it was for them. As with many refugees, language was a barrier to communication. According to Yang, it was not until her father used his limited English to explain to the sponsors that they had taken some food out to feed the children that they realized it had been intended for them all along. Her parents regretted not knowing sooner. They had waited until dinner every day to eat even though the kids were hungry.

Two sponsors in particular, Bob Schneider, whom they called "Uncle Bob," and a man her parents called "Johnson," were very active in helping their family. Uncle Bob visited them frequently and took the kids out to get ice cream at the local ice cream shop. He also took her family on picnics and drove them to visit other Hmong families who had arrived in Milwaukee. Johnson taught Yang's father how to count money, how to drive, and how to take the bus.

Yang's family practiced the animist religion upon arrival in Milwaukee. Sometime after Yang's extended family joined them in Milwaukee in the 1980s, the entire family decided to forgo animism for Christianity, so everyone started attending the Northwest Baptist Church in Milwaukee, where her uncle is a pastor.

Yang's family later moved to a house in Wauwatosa, Wisconsin. There, Yang began kindergarten at Roosevelt Elementary School with no English-language skills. Like other refugee children, Yang believed growing up that she was both the experiment and the experimenter. As the oldest child in her family, she became her parents' experiment. Like parents in any culture, they were learning how to parent effectively, but their job was made more difficult by being in an unfamiliar country. Similarly, Yang had to learn to navigate for her parents and younger siblings and to find the balance between her two worlds. As a Hmong girl, she felt pulled between two ideals: the more traditional view that she should behave, listen, and not be heard and a more modern vision of strength and independence.

After attending Steuben Middle School, Yang went to multiple high schools before she graduated. She transferred from Custer High School to James Madison High School to enroll in the gifted and talented program. However, when she arrived at James Madison, the coursework was so far ahead of where she had been at Custer, Yang felt lost. She went from being an A student to being a C student. She worked harder during study halls and always carried home a huge backpack filled with books.

At home, she tried to explain biology to her mom to reinforce what she had learned in class. By the end of the year, she had raised her grade point average.

In Yang's second year of high school, she realized her passion for programming and decided to enroll in computer science classes at Washington High School while still attending James Madison. The schools gave Yang very different personal experiences. James Madison had only one other Hmong student and, as a freshman, he was married. But many Hmong students attended Washington, some of whom were married and others who were not. Yang found she identified more with the married girls at the school. She enjoyed talking to them and learning about their lives, especially listening to the struggles they faced as young, married Hmong girls. Although only a year or so older, they seemed much more mature than she felt. They watched over Yang like a little sister, which Yang appreciated.

Fearing she would marry early like other Hmong teenagers, Yang's mother curbed her social life by not allowing her to stay after school for any activities. "I, on the other hand, was the typical 'nothing will happen to me' teenager," Yang recalled. "I didn't know what the big deal was. I knew being a housewife was not for me at that young age. I absolutely, without a doubt, knew I was going to college."

While she had her eyes set on college and a career, Yang still considers the influence of her family and her Hmong peers during those teen years to be significant in shaping the person she is today. Kalia S. Vang Lor, daughter of Pastor Neng Mai Sayaovong Vang, taught her grace, patience, and devotion. Yang remembers that when they started going to church, Kalia welcomed her into their house with an open and warm heart. Kalia taught Yang how to sing songs and how to be less fearful of everyone around her. Like others in her generation, Yang did not know how to read Hmong, so Kalia taught her. Yang's second cousin, Kao S. Violet, also was a role model. Yang recalls that Kao taught her how to be strong and to believe in herself.

Yang graduated third in her class from high school and received a scholarship to go to the University of Wisconsin–Madison. But after visiting the large campus, Yang declined because she knew it just was not for her, and she felt she would be lost. When she visited Carroll College (now Carroll University), she knew the smaller school would be the place she would call home for the next four years. In 1994, Yang graduated with a bachelor of science degree in computer science and a minor in psychology.

Yang shared the three things that motivated her to attend college: environment, family, and her husband. Growing up on the north side of Milwaukee, where few Hmong families resided, her exposure to Hmong families and customs was limited. The only other Hmong Yang associated with were her cousins, who shared her values and beliefs. Because of her environment, Yang did know that some Hmong girls got married young, but because her cousins and American peers did not, it never occurred to Yang to do so. She related more to the American culture, so she wanted the American dream: to finish high school with honors, graduate from college in four years with her own career, and then get married.

Having family support also motivated Yang to finish college. As in many other Hmong families, her parents worked hard and taught her to work hard too. Yang's mother worked during the day and her father worked during the night so that at least one parent was home to take care of the children. Her parents told her that they worked hard and dreamed big so that one day their children would not have to work as hard as they did. With such a vision in mind, the parents were very supportive of their children's education and encouraged them to attend and finish college.

Although it was not her goal to marry young, Yang happened to find the person she considers to be her soulmate in high school. "I started dating my husband in eleventh grade," she said. "We met at a leadership conference held at the University of Wisconsin–Madison. Both of us realized early on that one day we would be married but never felt pressured to get married. We could close our eyes and see each other in our futures." They encouraged each other to finish school. They felt secure and confident about the future. Therefore, their college years were not filled with distractions.

After college, Yang went to work, putting her information technology skills to work. She got married and started a family in Madison. Their family later moved to Sun Prairie. In 1998, after the company she worked for went out of business, Yang and her coworkers Melanie Gebauer and Bob Kube founded Titan Public Safety Solutions. Yang's company provides software for law enforcement agencies and municipal courts all across Wisconsin. Yang spoke passionately about her company and how her software helps municipalities all around the state.

❧❧

# SIA VANG (TXAWJ TXHIAJ VAJ)

*Sia Vang is an entrepreneur living in Appleton, where his family owned a video store. He was interviewed by the author.*

As I drove to Appleton to meet with Sia Vang, I thought a lot about my years in Kaukauna and Appleton. I knew and worked with Vang's older cousin and had served his uncle a few times due to my father's connections. But I could not remember any interaction with Vang himself besides at community picnics we had both attended at High Cliff State Park, where the elders had shared good food and laughter and parents had a chance to share stories about the cultural barriers they had met at work.

When I arrived midmorning, the video store had just opened, and both Vang and Mao Thao, his wife, were at the store. I stood by the cashier counter while Vang did his paperwork on the other side. A former CIA employee, he chose his words carefully and said only positive things at first. But as he warmed up, he shared many classic stories of heartache and perseverance, from the difficulties of being one of the first two Hmong families to arrive in Wisconsin to a busy and rewarding life operating their video store and enjoying the fruits of their labor—their children and grandchildren.

Vang's family and Tou Her's family arrived in Wisconsin together, but while Vang's family went to Appleton, Her's family continued on to Wausau. On January 31, 1976, Vang's sponsors, members of the Prince of Peace Lutheran Church, greeted him, his wife, and their son with coats and warm blankets and took them to their new home. Because he had worked for the USAID program in Laos during the Secret War, Vang understood about 20 percent of the English spoken upon his arrival. I was amazed to learn that English is Vang's fifth language.

Vang shared that he thought a lot about his new life on the long plane ride to America. He was especially worried about starvation, unsure whether he and his wife would have rice to eat and what they would do if they did not like the new foods provided by their sponsors. It was a huge relief to find two whole raw chickens in the refrigerator and a bag of rice sitting on the kitchen counter upon arrival at his new home.

Food was not the only thing Vang worried about in those early days.

Because it had been late evening when they arrived, they did not see much between the airport and their house. The next day, Vang woke up to see icy white stuff all over the ground outside. Disoriented and confused, he spent his first day wondering at the "white ice" on the ground and trying to figure out why he had not seen anyone walking outside during the daytime. The city seemed dead and cold. Curious, he repeatedly went outside and brought a handful of snow inside to study. Inside, he sat and watched the snow melt.

Unable to sleep while adjusting to the new time zone, the Vangs killed time that first day watching *Popeye* on television. On the second day, their sponsors came to visit and gave them a brief orientation about their new home and life, including the snow. On their third day, they went grocery shopping and purchased enough food to last a week. When Sunday arrived, the sponsors took them to church and introduced them to the congregation. After that introduction, Vang was amazed at the volume of incoming donations—clothes, canned foods, and other goods—that people dropped off for them.

As one of the first two Hmong refugee families in the state, Vang has carried a heavy load on his shoulders. He knew he was the bridge between the United States and the families still in the refugee camps in Thailand, so he worked hard to pave the way for others. His first two priorities were learning American currency and acquainting himself with the new environment. With a strong desire to learn, he mastered all the coins and bills within the first week. During the second week, Vang explored his new environment. "Back then, my method of memorizing my location—where my house was—was snow," he recalled, smiling. "I walked on the snow, not the sidewalk, so I could trace my footprints back to my house. I walked one block and traced my footprints home. I walked two blocks and then traced my footprint home again. I memorized the street names as I walked." When the weather was not so cold, he would go out a couple of times per day. In one week, he memorized most of the streets around his new home. After a week's worth of exploring the neighborhood, Vang no longer was afraid of his new environment. He could walk from his house to the old Kohl's store—now the Thompson Community Center—and back in fifteen minutes. After the first month, Vang had enough confidence to walk to the Kohl's grocery store to buy groceries and carry them home.

After three months of getting to know his way around, Vang started work as a janitor and dishwasher at the Country Inn Restaurant earning $2.25 per hour. He walked to work during the first few weeks until his sponsor gave him a bike. Regardless of how much snow was on the ground, Vang rode his bike to work. With a grin on his face, he said, "When there were a lot of snow and ice, I walked my bike home instead."

Feeling more secure in his home, job, and the assistance of his sponsors, Vang sent word to his relatives in the refugee camps to assure them that it was safe to come to the United States. Like others in the camps, his relatives had heard that *zaj* (dragons) waited to eat people in America. Vang sent many letters to his relatives detailing his new life and the opportunities he found here and encouraging them to come to Wisconsin so they could reunite as a family. His efforts resulted in most of his brothers and relatives joining him in Appleton two years later. Upon the arrival of his parents and relatives, he was no longer homesick and was able to concentrate on his new life as an American.

As Vang adjusted, he faced new challenges. One of the most frightening experiences for Vang as a new refugee was driving on unfamiliar roads. In Laos, he had driven while working for the USAID program as an employee of the CIA. After one month in Wisconsin, he was able to take the road test, and after six months, he received a temporary license to drive but did not know his way around. One day his sponsor took him to the Asian grocery store in Green Bay. On the way there, Vang secretly drew the directions on a piece of a napkin. He and his wife were very conservative with the fifty-pound bag of rice purchased on the trip, making just enough per meal, fearing they would not be able to get a new supply without their sponsors.

A month later, when they had run out of rice and their sponsors had not returned, Vang decided it was time to take out his handwritten map. He drove to Green Bay with his wife. "I drove slowly and carefully to Green Bay to buy a bag of rice," Vang said, laughing as he shared the story. "I followed my map carefully. I went on the highway for a long time before I entered the city of Green Bay. I entered a bridge and drove up. As I drove up, I saw cars coming ahead toward me. I backed up very quickly! I was so scared and frightened then. This was scarier than walking to work!"

Vang thinks of the sponsors and others who helped his family as angels. He said that an angel entered his life after he spent five months as a dishwasher. That person was a church member who owned his own roofing company and was a friend of Vang's official sponsor. The man hired Vang to do roofing and carpentry for him. The work was much harder, but the pay was much higher at $7.50 per hour. As a result, Vang began to save. In 1978, after a couple of years of hard work, Vang wanted a change, so he got a job at the Riverside Paper Company as a packager. After two years there, due to Vang's ability to troubleshoot and fix a problem when a machine broke down, he was promoted to a machine operator. With this promotion, he now earned $12.25 per hour. He worked at Riverside Paper Company until it closed in 1993.

Like other refugees, Vang sometimes faced racism or discrimination as he assimilated. For example, when he was promoted to machine operator, he recalls a coworker saying, "You came here and you took our jobs, so go back to your home." "I told him, 'We all work and pay taxes to the government. If you are not happy, you go speak to the government.'"

In 1978, after much hard work and saving, Vang became the first Hmong homeowner in Appleton when he purchased a house on Hancock Street for twenty-six thousand dollars. In 1981, he and his brothers purchased land on the south side of Appleton and, using the carpentry skills Vang had learned, built three houses so they all could live close together. In 1984, Vang opened an Asian video store on Wisconsin Avenue to address the homesickness of many Hmong refugees. By 1995, his wife went to work at Anchor Food while he stayed home to manage the video business.

Because he was the first to arrive and spoke more English, Vang became a leader and spokesperson for the Hmong in all service areas— helping out if someone had to go to the hospital or talk to the police or human services, for example. He was called to assist at all hours of the day and night. As more Hmong acclimated to life in Wisconsin and learned English, they took on some of these responsibilities.

Vang and his uncle, Youa True Vang, teamed up to serve the community around the Fox Cities area. Vang had the language skill, and his uncle was a well-known and well-respected clan leader who had worked closely with General Vang Pao in Laos. They and other Hmong leaders organized community picnics, meetings, and gatherings to identify and resolve any unmet needs. They developed community social services for Hmong refugees and pooled money to purchase a plane ticket to bring the former general to visit the Hmong in Wisconsin in 1977. They also spearheaded other efforts to help Hmong refugees adjust, including the Sunny Trust Fund to pay for funeral expenses and the Community Food Market, a local cooperative to sell Asian foods.

Vang found himself helping wherever there was a need. For example, one time he was waiting in line to pay for his groceries. The person ahead of him was a Hmong woman who did not have enough money, so he paid for the rest of her grocery bill. Another example was when Vang drove by and saw some Hmong visitors waiting at the Greyhound bus station. He did not know them, but he took them to his home. His wife served them dinner while Vang called their relatives to come pick them up.

Three decades after their arrival in Wisconsin, Sia Vang and Mao Thao are grandparents to eighteen grandchildren. Their English-language skills improved from a second-grade to a twelfth-grade level. They chose to stay in Appleton all their lives, while others have moved out of state and back. "We have not moved anywhere because, through consultation with a Thai friend in DC in our early years, we knew that wherever we went, we must work hard to feed ourselves and families," Vang said.

# SUGGESTED READINGS

Aleckson, Paul, Anne Jagodzinski, and James Kegel. *The Hmong and Their Stories*. Weston, WI: D.C. Everest Oral History Project, 2001.

Dao, Yang. *Hmong at the Turning Point*. Minneapolis: WorldBridge Associates, 1993.

Duffy, John. *Writing from These Roots: Literacy in a Hmong-American Community*. Honolulu: University of Hawaii Press, 2007.

Faderman, Lillian, with Ghia Xiong. *I Begin My Life All Over: The Hmong and the American Immigrant Experience*. Boston: Beacon Press, 1998.

Faruque, Cathleen Jo. *Migration of the Hmong to the Midwestern United States*. Lanham, MD: University Press of America, 2002.

Koltyk, Jo Ann. *New Pioneers in the Heartland: Hmong Life in Wisconsin*. Boston: Allyn and Bacon, 1998.

Moua, Mai Neng, ed. *Bamboo Among the Oaks: Contemporary Writing by Hmong Americans*. St. Paul: Minnesota Historical Society Press, 2002.

Pfaff, Tim. *Hmong in America: Journey from a Secret War*. Eau Claire, WI: Chippewa Valley Museum Press, 1995.

Vang, Chia Youyee. *Hmong America: Reconstructing Community in Diaspora*. Urbana: University of Illinois Press, 2010.

Yang, Kao Kalia. *The Latehomecomer: A Hmong Family Memoir*. Minneapolis: Coffee House Press, 2008.

# SELECTED BIBLIOGRAPHY

Ahern, Thomas L., Jr. *Undercover Armies: CIA and Surrogate Warfare in Laos.* Washington, DC: Center for the Study of Intelligence, 2006.

Associated Press. "Hunter Receives Life in Prison for Killing Six Men." *NBCNews.com,* 2013. www.nbcnews.com/id/9972929/ns/us_news-crime_and_courts/t/hunter-receives-life-prison-killing-six-men/#.W_Mc3DFRcrg.

Beck, Roy. "The Ordeal of Immigration in Wausau." *Atlantic Monthly* 273, no. 4 (1994): 84–97.

Dao, Yang. *Hmong at the Turning Point.* Minneapolis: WorldBridge Associates, 1993.

"Documentary Re-examines Controversial Hmong Shooting." *Tell Me More,* NPR, October 27, 2010. www.npr.org/templates/story/story.php?storyId=130860575.

Dougherty, Barbara, and Sarah Hendon. *Career Development with Hmong Women.* Madison: Center on Education and Work, 1995.

Hamilton-Merritt, Jane. *Tragic Mountains: The Hmong, the Americans, and the Secret Wars for Laos, 1942–1992.* Bloomington: Indiana University Press, 1993.

Her, Chong Lee, interview by Mai Zong Vue (August 18, 2011).

Hillmer, Paul. *A People's History of the Hmong.* St. Paul: Minnesota Historical Society Press, 2010.

Hmong National Development. *Focal Point: A Closer Look at Hmong Mutual Assistance Associations.* Washington, DC: Hmong National Development, 2002.

Koltyk, Jo Ann. *New Pioneers in the Heartland: Hmong Life in Wisconsin.* Boston: Allyn and Bacon, 1998.

Kong, Neng Yee, interview by Mai Zong Vue (April 2013).

Lee, Mai Na M. *Dreams of the Hmong Kingdom.* Madison: University of Wisconsin Press, 2015.

Lee, Stacey J. "The Road to College: Hmong American Women's Pursuit of Higher Education." *Harvard Educational Review* 67, no. 4: 803–28.

Līprīchā, Prasit, Suphāng Čhanthāwanit, and Thawin Phīansī. *The Lao Hmong in Thailand: State Policies and Operations (1975–2009).* Bangkok: Sriboon Computer-Printing, 2011.

Ly, My Thao, interview by Mai Zong Vue (October 29, 2009).

Malphurs, Aubrey. *Planting Growing Churches for the 21st Century.* Grand Rapids, MI: Baker Book House, 1992.

Mattison, Wendy, Laotou Lo, Thomas Scarseth, and Alfred Charles Bonanno. *Hmong Lives from Laos to La Crosse: Stories of Eight Hmong Elders*. La Crosse, WI: Pump House Regional Center for the Arts, 1994.

Moua, Houa V., interview by Mai Zong Vue (August 25, 2010).

Moua, Vayong. *Reflection of the 34th Anniversary of the Journey to America*. Unpublished manuscript, n.d.

Moua, Young Kay, interview by Mai Zong Vue (August 25, 2010).

Levine, Ken, and Ivory Waterworth Levine, directors. *Becoming American: The Odyssey of a Refugee Family*. Franklin Lakes, NJ: New Day Films, 1983.

Lee, Mai Na M. *Dreams of the Hmong Kingdom*. Madison: University of Wisconsin Press, 2015.

Nida, Eugene A. *Customs and Cultures*. Pasadena, CA: William Carey Library, 1954.

Office of Refugee Resettlement. *ORR Annual Report*. Washington, DC: Office of Refugee Resettlement, 1983.

Office of Refugee Resettlement. *Annual Report to Congress*. Washington, DC: Office of Refugee Resettlement, 1993.

Pfaff, Tim. *Hmong in America: Journey from a Secret War*. Eau Claire, WI: Chippewa Valley Museum Press, 1995.

Roop, Peter, and Connie Roop. *The Hmong in America: We Sought Refuge Here*. Appleton, WI: Appleton Area School District, 1990.

Schneider, Pat. "UW Efforts on Hmong Studies Don't Meet Expectations." *Madison Capital Times*, February 16, 2010.

Schofield, Steven, director. *A Brief History of the Hmong & the Secret War*. Milwaukee: Hmong American Friendship Association, 2004.

"Women's Motivational Workshop: Racist Comment/Actions Toward Hmong." July 25, 1991. In John D. Medinger Papers, La Crosse Area Research Center. www.wisconsinhistory.org/turningpoints/search.asp?id=1322.

Vandenberg, Father Robert Paul, interview by Mai Zong Vue (September 4, 2010).

Vang, Chia, interview by Mai Zong Vue (October 26, 2009).

Vang, Chia Youyee. *Hmong America: Reconstructing Community in Diaspora*. Urbana: University of Illinois Press, 2010.

Vang, Chia Youyee. "Making Ends Meet: Hmong Socioeconomic Trends in the U.S." *Hmong Studies Journal* 13, no. 2 (2012): 1–20.

Vang, Kou. *Portraits of Hmong Women: Photographic Documentary with Essay*. Milwaukee: Kou Vang, 2017.

Vang, Thomas S. *A History of the Hmong*. Vang, 2008.

Vang, Timothy T. *Coming Full Circle: Historical Analysis of the Hmong Church Growth 1950–1998*. Ann Arbor: UMI Company, 1999.

Vu, Doua H. *Remembering the Hmong*. Fresno: Fresno Unified School District, 2008.

Vue, Thai, interview by Mai Zong Vue (May 15, 2013).

"Wisconsin Vietnam War Stories." Wisconsin Public Television, May 25, 2010. Video, 58:41, wpt.org/Wisconsin-War-Stories/vietnam-war-stories/sponsors.

*Wisconsin's Hmong Population, Census 2000 Population, and Other Demographic Trends*. Madison: University of Wisconsin Extension and Applied Population Laboratory, 2003.

Xiong, Ghia, and Lillian Faderman. *The Hmong and the American Immigrant Experience: I Begin My Life All Over*. Boston: Beacon Press, 1998.

Xiong, Victor, interview by Mai Zong Vue (2012).

Yang, Touhoua. "Who Are We? Who Am I?" *InSight*. Madison: Hmong American Students Association, March 31 and April 1, 2006.

Yang, Xia Vue, interview by Mai Zong Vue (December 9, 2013).

Zaniewski, Kazimierz J., and Carol J. Rosen. *The Atlas of Ethnic Diversity in Wisconsin*. Madison: University of Wisconsin Press, 1998.

# ACKNOWLEDGMENTS

This book would not be possible without the support of my husband, CherPeng, who often replaced me in the kitchen so I could hide at my desk, and of my children, especially my older daughter. At first, Nongnah kept asking, "Are you done with your book yet?" Then a couple of years later, she said, "Mom, you have children, you should not write a book!" Not only was I frustrated as the writing process took longer than I anticipated, but my daughter was frustrated on my behalf. Nongnah saw the balancing act of writing in my spare time, raising a young family, working full-time, developing and advocating for Hmong studies and language programs, and dealing with the declining health and loss of my mother in the course of writing this book.

I have learned so much about the disciplined process of writing, and I am thankful for everyone who supported me throughout these years. I would like to give a big thank you to my dear friend Dia Cha, PhD, for her ongoing support and guidance. Dia was more than an adviser and counselor throughout the process. A shout-out goes to Chia Vang, PhD, at the University of Wisconsin–Milwaukee, for her initial encouragement.

No words can express the appreciation and support I received from all the Hmong community leaders, including Xia Vang, Victor Xiong, Yong Kay Moua, and Neng Yee Kong, whom I have interviewed for this book. A special thanks is in order for Charles Lor, Xong Yang, and Yee Thao for sharing their personal stories. These individuals not only shared their stories in great length but also provided many pictures— although I have not been able to include all of them in this book. From the bottom of my heart, thank you for your kind hearts, love, and support for Hmong refugees and this book!

Lastly, thank you to the leadership and staff of the Wisconsin Historical Society Press for adding the Hmong story to its People of Wisconsin series. Most important, thanks for the support and understanding throughout the lengthy process, especially during the loss of my mother. I will always treasure that day when the staff from the Wisconsin Historical Society Press approached me at Taste of Asia about this Hmong project. It was an honor to write this book, given that I used to go to the Wisconsin Historical Museum to check whether a book about the Hmong had yet appeared next to those about other ethnic groups. Thank you, Wisconsin Historical Society, for your inclusiveness and leadership.

# THE AUTHOR

Born in the middle of the Secret War in Bouam Long, Laos, Mai Zong Vue left Laos in May 1975 with her family for Thailand as the Communists took over the Lao government. After almost five years in the refugee camps, Mai Zong arrived with her family in 1980 in Illinois through a church sponsor and relocated to Wisconsin to join her oldest sister's family. As the first in her family to graduate from college, Mai Zong received her undergraduate degree from Lakeland College (now Lakeland University) and her master's degree from the University of Wisconsin–Madison in 1997.

In her twenty-plus years with the Wisconsin State Refugee Office, Mai Zong was the Refugee Program Specialist, where she developed the Refugee Family Strengthening Program to address domestic abuse. Her advocacy and grassroots activism helped lead to the development of nonprofit agencies in Wisconsin and Georgia to provide human services to Hmong and refugee women; women's empowerment and leadership training for refugee women; the creation of a Hmong Studies position at UW–Madison; the Hmong Language and Culture Enrichment Program; and the Hmong Institute. She has received several honors for her efforts in serving communities in need, including the YWCA of Dane County's Women of Distinction Leadership Award, Authentic Hmong Leaders, and International Women's Day Trailblazer.

Mai Zong continues to serve the Hmong in Wisconsin in different capacities. She works for the Wisconsin Department of Health Services while enjoying her children and spending her free time as a community advocate, an educator on Hmong culture, and a folklore performer.

# INDEX

97